Where is the FKN Commonsense?

Dr. M. Asif Nawaz

authorHOUSE®

AuthorHouse™
1663 Liberty Drive
Bloomington, IN 47403
www.authorhouse.com
Phone: 833-262-8899

Published by AuthorHouse 08/12/2024

ISBN: 979-8-8230-3191-2 (sc)
ISBN: 979-8-8230-3190-5 (e)

Library of Congress Control Number: 2024916914

Print information available on the last page.

The Author Is a Proud American.

A true patriot must be courageous in speaking the truth to their fellow citizens. In today's world, discussing sensitive issues that impact the broader community often makes people uncomfortable. However, addressing these topics openly is crucial, as it fosters awareness and paves the way for solutions. Everyone's civic duty is to enhance our nation's institutions by being objective and transparent. This book advocates for a commonsense approach, offering valuable suggestions that resonate with many. Yet, fear of repercussions from vested interests, political affiliations, religious beliefs, career aspirations, and generational biases often stifles open dialogue. As Americans, we are fortunate to have the freedom of speech, a powerful tool to improve our system through constructive criticism and thoughtful recommendations. Your voice is crucial in this process. This freedom sets us apart from many other societies and oppressive, fascist, isolationist, and dictatorial regimes. Let us harness this right to fortify our nation.

Let our fellow citizens decide if this book makes sense, and "enough is enough?"

CONTENTS

AN UNCONVENTIONAL BOOK

About This Book – A Must Read

Many whisper comments like, "Politicians, policymakers, and leaders don't really care about me," "Speeches and promises are just for ratings and show," and "It seems things in the U.S. are deteriorating at a rapid rate." These rumors and gossip should be troublesome for policymakers and politicians, but are they listening, or are they in their own bubble, hearing only what they want to hear?

Many of my friends often ask why some politicians and policymakers create polarization in today's climate of traditional news, social media frenzy, and media gossip. Why don't they use common sense and simplify things? Conversely, why do many make things more complex?

People who ask commonsense questions receive responses like: "You don't know what's happening behind the scenes," "It's above your pay grade," "Don't worry about this—it won't affect us," "It's not your job," "Things are not that simple," "You are racist," "You are dumb," "The government is listening; you may get into trouble," "The deep state doesn't want you to talk about this," "Politicians do what lobbyists and corporations want them to do," "You don't have the security clearance to know this," and "You won't get a job if you talk about this." Many believe that today's policymakers and politicians don't have time to listen or read beyond three lines and seem interested only in their personal ambitions.

The excuse of national security and behind-the-scenes complexity provides perfect cover for those seeking to exploit insecurities, biases, fears, and self-fulfilling prophecies, bypassing objectivity, critique, and timely accountability. I feel some people complicate issues to their advantage, much like the case of illegal immigration. The U.S. is a nation of immigrants. To me, the problem is not illegal immigration but the lack of strict enforcement of the current laws and real consequences. If the law were properly enforced, would caravans of illegal immigrants keep coming? Some argue for humanity and compassion over the law, neglecting that law and order protect humanity. Coming to this country the proper and legal way, standing in line like millions who have done so, is necessary. Turning a blind eye to illegal immigration penalizes and discriminates against those who follow the proper process and patiently wait to join this great nation; in fact, our policymakers should make the system more transparent and efficient (timelier) for those who want to come the proper way to contribute positively to this nation's development.

To many, some leaders appear highly selfish, working only for their self-interest, mindlessly following the trends of their inner circles, careers, promotions, and photo-ops instead of standing up for what is right. It seems that moral values nowadays are limited to personal preferences and used as a talk and a showcase for books, ratings, shows, and fake image building. Self-interest is not bad unless it erodes conscience, human compassion, and the ability to differentiate between right and wrong—attributes that distinguish humans from animals. We all go to our own graves; at least, we should be honest with our own souls. Some don't believe in afterlife accountability or karma. When private monetary gains, job security, political affiliations, preconceived biases, and generational memories take precedence over objectivity, national interests, and ethical values, society's moral fabric begins to deteriorate, affecting institutions and, eventually, the nation. As a result, many of my American friends are worried about ongoing issues in America and worldwide.

The disconnect between traditional policymakers, wealthy politicians, and everyday hardworking Americans is growing at an alarming rate. To the ordinary person, our leaders seem more concerned with giving aid, rescuing other nations, and strengthening foreign democracies with taxpayer money. They are fighting others' wars with our resources and sacrificing our soldiers. But what benefits does the average Joe receive from these actions? While we bolster democracies abroad, are we neglecting our own democracy and human rights, thus becoming more divided by the day? Why aren't we first investing our taxpayer money in our roads, schools, hospitals, industries, healthcare, law enforcement, and institutions? These perceptions point to a growing mistrust, frustration, and lack of faith in our system. It's a rat race, and most people never realize how greed erodes inner peace and how karma eventually settles scores. Instead of focusing on U.S. growth, development, and success, the current trend seems to emphasize countering rivals' propaganda and building other nations. Do those we help pay taxes to the U.S. government? This disconnect is a clarion call for change, urging us to prioritize our own nation's needs and ensure that the hardworking Americans who sustain this country benefit from their government's actions.

Did we build a peaceful and stable Iraq, Libya, Syria, Afghanistan, etc.? Did we stabilize those countries or leave them in more chaos? With all these efforts, why is anti-American sentiment rising worldwide, and frustrations at home increasing? At home, do we identify more by political party, race, religion, etc., or do we identify as Americans? Something seems very off to me.

Amid these perceptions and discussions, pre- and post-COVID developments, and economic concepts, this book bluntly addresses what people are reluctant to discuss due to political incorrectness. Even if the problem affects them, many are unwilling to speak openly about the real issues. Is it the economy and unemployment? Is it the fight over resources to secure future insecurities, ironically making us more insecure by the day? Is it something about securing eternity per generational religious beliefs? Is there a need for more will to enforce the law? Or are those regional, generational animosities affecting our decision-making and thought processes? Or is it just a self-centered attitude, mindless greed, hypocrisy, and lack of common sense?

To answer the above QUESTIONS, i.e., what is the real problem and if there are any practical solutions? This book has some common-sense analysis and concepts with recommendations for those seriously looking for practical solutions to issues that some of our politicians need help solving/implementing. This book is a different type of book for everyday people and decision-makers, politicians, policymakers, bureaucrats, intelligence, and the intelligentsia, asking if we are using common sense to unconditionally uphold the basic tenets of ethics and the supreme law of the land.

Common sense is becoming a rare commodity. This book will have very few references and no bibliography; common sense doesn't require many references. Readers can decide if they agree with the analysis using their common sense. Policymakers and politicians limited to a three-line psyche may not have time to read references anyway. Readers can use common sense to agree or disagree with this book.

People sometimes speak without thinking. Sometimes, they are reluctant to say the right thing because it is politically incorrect. This paradox happens at almost every level of society. Ego, self-interest, race, color, religion, and party affiliations dominate logic and common sense. Additionally, most people seem overworked, with limited time to think deeply beyond watching the news and using social media.

Consider the January 6, 2021, riots. I am against any riots and lawlessness. If someone breaks the law, justice should be done. The U.S. Constitution is the "supreme law of the land." But nobody asks why the rioters rioted. That many people cannot be crazy. Why were so many people frustrated enough to riot? Is that something to do with their education, media poisoning, not knowing right from wrong, or some problem with the system? There is something terribly wrong with this picture. Why not first fix the issues that made those people feel helpless and frustrated, triggering their patriotic feelings and leading them to extreme measures? This question and many others led me to write this commonsense book.

Initially, I planned to write a traditional book with a foreword, preface, references, bibliography, etc., discussing the January 6 riots and factors like economics, unemployment, prosperity, crime rate, and frustration with the status quo, along with some recommendations. I also wanted to highlight a developmental economics article, "Space Economics," addressing solutions to ongoing civic, economic, and unemployment issues. This project could lead to a multi-trillion-dollar industry promoting world peace and collaboration, rescuing COVID-affected economies. Visionaries like Elon Musk and Richard Branson could initiate such projects, changing geopolitics forever, beyond traditional policymakers' comprehension.

When I shared this book idea with a close friend, he said the issues and questions are valid, but nobody would read such a book—many people write this kind of book. His advice prompted me to write a commonsense book. I don't need to follow the traditional way. Using commonsense should make things simple, not complicated. Many people hear these issues daily and wonder why no one can fix them. This book creates awareness and may offer commonsense tips for policymakers, leaders, and architects of our system to go beyond the three-line mentality and do some soul-searching, including the "Space Economics" idea for their consideration. The concept promotes a vision of collaboration, exploring beyond traditional economics and current policymakers' trends, aligning with the American spirit of thinking outside the box, taking risks, and being original.

This book will discuss controversial topics with straightforward analysis and suggestions that may not align with mainstream media's political correctness. After the section "Points to Ponder: Ask These Questions to Yourself First," there are some additional random thought-provoking topics people are uncomfortable discussing openly. These topics may encourage readers to start dialogues on important issues with a commonsense approach, potentially leading to critical thresholds for commonsense and straightforward solutions. Unfortunately, simple, commonsense suggestions may seem complicated or foolish to highly qualified and experienced experts, and some powerbrokers may lack the backbone to implement simple solutions.

Too many behind-the-scenes lobbyists and pressure groups often have agendas that conflict with ordinary citizens' benefits and even national interests, making commonsense solutions challenging to implement. Ordinary, straightforward taxpayers don't have the resources to counter lobbyists, pressure groups, or corporations. I request you to start asking commonsense questions instead of blindly listening to the news and politicians. Shouldn't our taxpayers' money be spent first on our own citizens' needs instead of democratizing other nations, unconditionally supporting friends and allies, giving enormous aid, foreign nation-building, and catering to corporate and lobbyist interests? Let's stop complicating things and start using commonsense solutions for everyday people; this will be a short, common-sense book for all.

NOTE: Space economics can be considered a branch of developmental economics, particularly as it pertains to the development of new industries, technologies, and markets related to space. Developmental economics traditionally focuses on improving the economic conditions of regions or countries (particularly developing countries), often addressing issues like poverty, infrastructure, and industrial growth.

Space economics extends these concepts into the realm of outer space, encompassing the development and commercialization of space-related activities such as satellite communications, space tourism, asteroid mining, and even the colonization of other planets. This new frontier presents unique opportunities and challenges for economic development, potentially driving innovation, creating jobs, and generating wealth in ways that can transform both developed and developing economies.

Therefore, while space economics has its own distinct characteristics and focus, it shares many principles and objectives with developmental economics, particularly in terms of fostering economic growth and improving living standards.

POINTS TO PONDER: ASK YOURSELF THESE QUESTIONS FIRST?

Hybrid Warfare on America and Americans?

The political polarization in America is growing, with the divide between right-wing and left-wing ideologies widening. Instead of thinking like Americans, many now primarily identify as Democrats or Republicans, Christians or Agnostics, and more. This division makes the nation vulnerable to hybrid propaganda and $5^{th}/6^{th}$ Generation warfare tactics employed by its rivals.

It's crucial to create awareness of how American enemies might be exploiting these divisions. By inciting contentious ideologies and fostering hopelessness, they are manipulating our unity. Americans should be cautious and not react impulsively to rumors and news that could be orchestrated by rivals. We must remain vigilant and not let our enemies sow discord. Issues like illegal immigration and drug abuse have straightforward solutions rooted in law enforcement and adherence to the rule of law.

If Americans succumb to enemy propaganda and make decisions based on emotions and gossip, they risk ignoring their Constitution and sidelining the rule of law—exactly what their enemies want. American values revolve around freedom, tolerance, justice, and

7

human rights. However, rivals may weaponize these strengths, turning limitless liberty into intolerance, defiance, laziness, fear, hate, suspicion, and chaos.

Hybrid warfare and stealth propaganda aim to divide nations, destabilize economies, promote chaos, and empower rival nations. Isn't it time to implement legislation to ensure accurate reporting by media outlets and to hold those who incite public discord for ratings accountable? Only our enemies and criminals benefit from this divide and hopelessness.

Why Aren't We Focusing on Our Own Problems?

Instead of concentrating on our law, order, and crime rates, we focus on stabilizing other countries. Rather than highlighting crime, violence, and danger abroad, we should focus on reducing our crime rates and violence. Many Americans view many Afghans in Afghanistan as violent and stubborn. Despite nearly every Afghan household possessing at least one AK-47, they don't experience school shootings or gun violence like we do in the U.S. Instead of banning guns, why don't we investigate factors like violent video games, the effects of drugs, early detection of behavioral issues, finding the real reasons behind shootings, and proactive law enforcement intervention?

We should fix our deteriorating infrastructure instead of developing other countries' infrastructure. Instead of building and modernizing schools overseas, we should focus on improving our own educational system. Rather than emphasizing education and skill-building in other countries, we should educate our own citizens to reduce the need for H1B visas and foreign workers.

Instead of addressing human rights violations and child marriages elsewhere, we should focus on our own issues. Many people are unaware of the statistics on child marriage in the U.S. (https://www.unchainedatlast.org/united-states-child-marriage-problem-study-findings-april-2021/). Instead of addressing our problems with racism and discrimination, we focus on teaching equality and fairness to others. Look at the hate, anti-Semitism, anti-minority, anti-Muslim, and even anti-white sentiments and incidents in the U.S. Instead of preaching equality, religious tolerance, and anti-discrimination to others, we should fix our issues first.

We live in a culture driven by ratings, corporate interests, influential lobbyists, and media hype. As a result, we are scared to acknowledge and address some issues due to party lines and political correctness.

Is President Trump Really Right?

To many, President Trump is a controversial figure. Some hate and dislike his guts, while others love and follow him. Some believe Trump is right, and others think otherwise.

Is President Trump right? Nobody is perfect, but he is right in many things, and he knows the pulse of the struggling working class better than any other politician. In many ways, I see him as a patriotic American, a corporate genius, and an effective President that is respected and appreciated by a large majority of the hardworking American labor force; otherwise, he wouldn't have received so many votes. President Trump understands the problems of everyday Americans and effectively puts those issues in the limelight, which others couldn't. Additionally, others did not use common gimmicks that effectively influenced and attracted ordinary people by suggesting simple, commonsense solutions to ongoing problems, which appealed to frustrated Americans. President Trump's genius marketing skills, which I greatly admire, played a significant role in his success.

While I may disagree with some of his language during campaigns, I admire and respect him for many things. By the way, what is wrong with some of the things that President Trump says or believe:

9

1. What is wrong with stopping illegal immigration and enforcing the law?
2. What is wrong with securing our borders?
3. What was wrong with making peace with Russia and collaborating on future economic development projects before the Ukrainian crisis?
4. What is wrong with asking allies to contribute fairly and not penalize U.S. taxpayers for defending those who don't prioritize American interests?
5. What is wrong with having a level playing field with China on tariffs?
6. What is wrong with vetting immigrants to counter threats and ensuring they assimilate into American culture?
7. What is wrong with building our infrastructure, prioritizing America first, and stopping aid to other countries where it often ends up in the hands of corrupt leaders?
8. What is wrong with limiting H1B visas and training our American youth for high-tech and medical jobs? Senators and education policymakers talk about reforming education but seldom experience the real problems firsthand. The easy way out is to expedite H1B visas instead of training our own.
9. Yes, law enforcement agencies should have checks and balances, and racism/discrimination should have no place in a civilized society. But what is wrong with empowering our law enforcement agencies and enforcing law and order to protect our citizens and businesses? We may need to embed social workers, mental health counselors, and behavioral therapists with law enforcement officers.
10. What is wrong with openly saying "Merry Christmas" and displaying a Christmas tree publicly?

We stress other nations' rights, freedom of speech, and religion, yet we are reluctant to say "Merry Christmas" openly at work in many places. What kind of freedom of speech and religion is that? If it is Christmas, we should say "Merry Christmas"; if it's Hanukkah, we should say "Happy Hanukkah"; if it's Eid, we should say "Happy Eid"; and if it's Diwali, we should say "Happy Diwali." If someone wishes me "Merry Christmas," I can respond in kind even if I am not a Christian. If someone doesn't celebrate Christmas, they can politely decline, but there's no need for a big fuss. I don't care what others think of it; they can mind their own business. If I celebrate Eid, I can invite my Christian, Hindu, Jewish, and atheist friends to join in the festivities. If they are uncomfortable, that's fine. I will still celebrate and extend invitations for others to join in my happiness.

What Benefits Are Our Taxpayers Getting from Giving Aid to Foreign Countries?

What benefits do hardworking American taxpayers, such as truck drivers and factory workers, receive from their hard-earned tax money sent as U.S. aid to countries worldwide? The citizens of these recipient countries do not pay taxes to the U.S., and often, the aid intended for development and assistance ends up in the wrong hands. Despite our assistance, anti-American sentiment seems to be on the rise in many of these nations. Moreover, when the U.S. provides unconditional support and aid to some allies who use that aid to subdue their rivals, those rivals—who were once friendly or neutral to the U.S.—become America's new enemies. This occurs because some of our allies use U.S. aid and support to harm these rivals, leading to resentment against America. We should not interfere in every other nation's business; instead, let those nations sort out their issues among themselves without our interference. This dilemma indicates that something is fundamentally wrong with our approach.

Why aren't we investing our taxpayer money in our roads, hospitals, healthcare, law enforcement, and institutions? Instead of focusing on U.S. growth, development, and success, the current trend emphasizes countering rivals' propaganda and building other nations. Whether it is Israel, Ukraine, Egypt, or other countries, we need to ask: what benefit do our factory workers, struggling citizens, and ordinary Americans get from these countries? On March 26, 2024, at 1:28 AM EDT, the Francis Scott Key Bridge in Baltimore, Maryland, collapsed after being struck by a container ship. Officials hope to rebuild it by 2028. Before sending aid abroad or building bridges overseas, let's focus on fixing our own, first. Prioritize American infrastructure to show that our people come first. Rebuild this bridge first before sending any aid to other countries to prove our commitment to domestic needs. American aid should start at home. Let's fix our own backyard first; it's about proving that America puts its citizens first.

Our taxpayers' money is being used to develop and assist other nations while our own needs remain unmet. Why not allocate those funds to provide quality and more affordable healthcare, reduce the cost of education for American students, and invest in our communities? The priority should be to address the challenges and needs of our citizens before extending help abroad. It is essential to create a robust and prosperous America that can effectively support its people.

Consider this: Instead of sending $61 billion in aid to Ukraine, $26 billion to Israel, and around $8 billion to U.S. allies in the Indo-Pacific region to counter China, why not invest that money in improving our healthcare system? Countries like Canada, the UK, Germany, and Australia offer affordable, universally accessible healthcare. We can do the same, ensuring that quality healthcare is available to every American at low rates. (aid figures are taken from the AP news link - https://apnews.com/article/ukraine-aid-israel-gaza-taiwan-c0645ad3 f47f9d919c8988a98593e887).

Why do selfish politicians and biased media try to mold affordable healthcare into socialism or something that can lead to a deteriorating healthcare system and quality of care? If those who speak against this healthcare system get into a severe health situation, I would ask them about their socialism and deteriorating healthcare logic. Have some sense and think beyond your selfish, self-centered, greedy, and narrow mentality.

Here's the reality: Americans are struggling with high medical costs and limited access to quality care. Our taxpayer money should prioritize the health and well-being of our citizens. Imagine the improvements we could make in our healthcare system with the $95 billion we send abroad. This funding could make healthcare more affordable and accessible, drastically improving the quality of life for millions of Americans.

A Simple Solution: With this level of investment, along with a potential 2% healthcare tax, we could establish a robust, affordable healthcare system. Americans might willingly contribute an additional 2% in taxes if it meant accessible, high-quality healthcare for everyone.

Uniform Healthcare Access: If a U.S. driver's license or passport can be used as an I.D. anywhere in the country, and a Wells Fargo or Bank of America check can be cashed nationwide, why shouldn't a healthcare card be just as universally accepted? We are the United States of America, after all. It's time our healthcare system reflects our unity and shared commitment to each other's well-being.

Harnessing Our Brainpower: Our senators and their staff are quick to mobilize resources and strategies for international aid. Imagine if that same brainpower and dedication were directed toward creating an affordable, uniform healthcare system for Americans. We have the intellectual resources and capability to make this a reality.

Investing in America means ensuring that our roads are safe, our schools are well-funded, our hospitals are equipped to provide quality care, and our industries are thriving. It means providing law enforcement with the necessary resources to maintain peace and security and ensuring our institutions are strong and capable. By prioritizing these areas, we can build a nation that stands resilient against external threats and internal challenges alike.

The Bottom Line: By reallocating funds and focusing on domestic healthcare, we can vastly improve the quality of life for American citizens and, in turn, improve our nation's longevity and resilience. It's time to prioritize our own people and ensure that every American has access to affordable, high-quality healthcare.

In conclusion, it is time to reevaluate our foreign aid policies and refocus our efforts on building a stronger, more prosperous

America. Our hardworking taxpayers deserve to see their money invested in their own future and well-being. By doing so, we can create a nation that supports its citizens and sets a positive example for the rest of the world.

Are Qualified and Suitable Candidates Even Coming Forward?

I once asked a retired U.S. General why he didn't run for elections or public office. I saw him as a sensible, qualified, and courageous individual who could competently address our issues. He responded that politics wasn't his "cliché." I was disappointed. When things aren't going well or adversely affect us, we often hear comments like, "Some people in power don't know what they are doing," or "The person in power is not competent or qualified." Many ridicule senators and some of our representatives.

We should not complain about the people in power making policies for us if we are reluctant to run for any public/government office ourselves. Three movies/documentaries, *Don't Look Up*, *Saving Capitalism*, and *Rotten*, have left me pondering this very issue. They all depict the consequences of greed and the void left when capable individuals shy away from competing in civil political leadership. Their absence is a loss we can't afford. It's crucial for capable and qualified individuals to come forward and participate in our political process. Only then can we hope to see real change and effective leadership.

When Will We Address Our Declining Education Standards and Student Behavior?

Some of us are highly concerned about the increasing disturbing student behavior. Beyond issues like drugs, bullying, and gun violence, the frequent use of foul language is becoming the norm. In many schools, students curse proudly in the hallways and classrooms without remorse, exhibiting a careless, indifferent attitude toward academics and ignoring teachers' and staff's directions. Cell phone use in classrooms, regardless of teachers' directions, is also out of control. The lack of accountability for rules and the freedom without boundaries or stricter consequences make things worse, reflecting the rifts in our polarized society. Many students have a "whatever, I don't care" attitude.

Our officials may need to realize that the problem is not just on our doorsteps but in our homes now. It is a ticking time bomb. Many students don't care about the consequences of not doing their homework or classwork. We are preparing an army of incompetent workers, a future that doesn't care, and citizens with an apathetic attitude towards authority and the country. How can the United States compete with citizens like this in the League of Nations? We must correct this problem now while the students are young. It is easier to grow strong children than to fix broken men.

Public schools and every individual school have specific rules, procedures, and student handbooks explaining the consequences and a moral code of conduct. But what good is suspension if it is considered a holiday for some students? Our education standards are declining, and gun violence and drug problems are increasing. President Lincoln imposed a type of virtual martial law to save the Union. Perhaps imposing a virtual martial law on towns and schools infested with drugs will clean up the mess before it takes over the country. If measures from Congress, law enforcement, and other government branches haven't fixed the ongoing problem by now, it means the traditional methods are not working, and we need a creative or firm solution.

Education will be productive if the primary focus is human-oriented, on moral values and ethics, not just money and stomach-oriented. If the primary focus were on money and stomach, the names of the wealthiest people in history would be more famous than Jesus, Moses, and Muhammad (PBUH). Instead, education should be skills-oriented, making citizens productive and proud to help their fellow citizens instead of seeking profit, lying, and fleecing others. Note: "Stomach-oriented" refers to focusing solely on practical or material needs, or merely working to obtain food for survival without any purpose.

As a progressive society, we need to fix our fundamentals. If the foundation is crooked, the whole building is at risk, no matter how good the materials used to construct it. Perhaps the laws we made to protect the innocent now protect the culprits more. Maybe there is less profit in fixing our schools and drug-infested cities than in waging wars, or for some lobbyists and big corporations. When our schools and education system are on the right track, we won't need H1B visas, we won't hire foreign workers, and we won't complain about foreigners taking jobs.

What can a teacher, an administrator, or a county official do when most students don't want to learn and don't care about the consequences? In some places, students have an "I don't care" attitude. *You can lead a horse to water, but you can't make it drink.* In inner-city schools, proactive and sincere efforts from officials are fruitless due to a lack of practical consequences. Students' behavioral problems grow because of a lack of effective authority and poor enforcement of strict and uniformed rules, laws, and procedures that tackle these issues effectively.

Our schools and students are a ticking time bomb because parents and teachers lack real, enforceable authority to discipline students to make them proactive, civilized, and productive. How can the United States compete like this in the League of Nations? If we don't fix our schools, the drug problems, and declining education standards, we won't compete efficiently and gracefully in the world. Most people don't run red lights because they know there are real consequences. Authority and law enforcement are deterrents to chaos and ensure a civilized life.

Lack of interest in learning, get-rich-quick attitudes, not knowing the difference between right and wrong, and not understanding the importance of the pledge of allegiance are not good indicators. Critics often blame teachers, substitutes, and staff, suggesting hiring new teachers with higher standards. But changing teachers won't fix the problem. The primary issue is students' behavior, attitudes, and unlimited rights without discipline.

Other shortcuts, like medicating behavioral students or labeling them bipolar, are more beneficial to pharmaceutical companies than solving the problem. These measures are like painkillers that suppress symptoms without addressing the cause. Some people believe that student behavior reflects how they are raised at home. Children need to be taught the difference between right and wrong.

Like ads creating awareness about drugs and smoking, the state could run campaigns about civic duties and moral values to foster a culture of respect, tolerance, peace, and law-abiding behavior. Sometimes, these campaigns exist, but they must be more appealing to new generations. Teachers and parents are afraid of the system and cannot enforce good values; this is how great empires decline. Critics should visit schools, observe students, and try teaching for a few weeks to understand the challenges. High-level consultants, senators, and politicians don't teach in failing schools daily. The teacher turnover rate is high in troubled schools. In some schools, good students who come to learn cannot learn due to the environment and peer pressure.

These students are our future workforce. We will see the effects on our workforce if we don't fix the system. We can focus on high tech, intelligence, military might, and economic strength to counter our rivals, but who will run these effectively? Sometimes, it's not the gun but the person behind it that makes the difference.

Are There Limitations to Democracy? Should We Revisit the Democracy Manual?

Democracy is often hailed as the best form of governance, but in my analysis, it requires certain prerequisites to thrive. If most people are intolerant, biased, and uneducated, influenced more by personal preferences than national interests, it can lead to what Plato described as "democracy is the right divine of the ignorant to rule ignorantly." Democracy can only thrive if 100% of the adult population is required to vote mandatorily. Additionally, democracy flourishes when at least 60-70% of voters are educated, understand the geopolitical arena and economic issues, and are well-informed about the personal life, character, and dealings of the officials running for election.

Why isn't democracy thriving in some countries where we are trying to establish it? Is it due to low literacy rates, lack of education, honest people not coming forward, democracy is becoming more like a business, the majority not voting, or people are voting blindly, or are they influenced by personal biases and generational perceptions?

The Influence of Ideologies and Manipulation: Some liberals have brainwashed the world with slogans of equality and freedom, while some conservatives have instilled fear and hate of anything different. Some politicians and kingmakers manipulate human emotions, exploiting insecurities to control the masses for their political ambitions and personal benefits. In many countries, religious elites further pollute the essence of democracy. Most people do not read their holy books or understand their religious fundamentals, allowing preachers to interpret religion based on their preferences and hidden ideologies. Many preachers and mullahs rewrite religion through their interpretations as if trying to teach religion to God Almighty.

The Role of Intelligence Agencies: Intelligence agencies should be unbiased and objective, ensuring unqualified, greedy, and wrong people do not come to power. If intelligence officials follow their personal and political preferences, the consequences can be exponentially disastrous. Why isn't such carelessness considered high treason or betrayal to the nation?

Historical Perspectives on Democracy: Would China, the USSR, and Great Britain have become significant powers if they had democracy from the start? Would many Middle Eastern countries be stable with absolute democracy? Despite their brutality, were Saddam Hussein's and Muammar Gaddafi's countries safer, more stable, and economically better off than they are now? How many refugees and illegal immigrants have been created due to these changes? Hitler was elected through a democratic process; would a 100% poll of Iraq and Libya's population show better conditions before or after these dictators?

Beyond Democracy and Capitalism: A nation needs more than just freedom, democracy, and capitalism to succeed. Unity, order, discipline, respect for others, hard work, integrity, a merit-based system, law enforcement, an impartial judiciary, a well-equipped military, investment in education, research and development, and efficient logistics are essential.

Current Political Climate: Instead of collaborating for national interests and humanity, many parliaments and congresses are fighting for right-wing and left-wing agendas. Parties often oppose anything good proposed by rivals without thinking. This divisive approach transforms the democratic process into an intellectual brothel of civility in the name of democracy, security, and freedom. It prioritizes personal interests over national interests, demonizes those who look or speak differently, and protects hidden agendas under the guise of rights and freedom. Yet, we still perceive ourselves as civilized creatures of the 21st century.

In Conclusion: We must revisit our understanding of democracy, address its limitations, and strive for a system that genuinely represents and benefits all citizens. Only by fostering education, unity, and integrity can we hope to achieve a truly thriving democracy.

Did the Russians Intervene in the Hillary vs. Trump Election?

Are we becoming like some politicians in developing countries, where we blame everything but ourselves for our defeat? Let's use some common sense: if Russia interfered, are Americans so easily swayed by foreign propaganda that it could change their votes?

President Trump ran a brilliant marketing campaign against a traditional political campaign. He used technology and strategy like a smart businessman and won. Many Democrats I knew didn't even vote because they believed Hillary would easily win; they thought their single vote wouldn't matter. On the other hand, Trump supporters, fed up with the status quo, made sure to cast their votes.

Now, let's look at President Trump losing the second term. He did well, but some of his actions distanced him from minority voters, energized Democrats, and motivated many undecided voters to oppose him. Many minorities believed he could strengthen America economically and bring law, order, and stability, but they also became scared of him. His marketing strategy worked but was undermined by his own actions. Even so, he performed well, and now, as he runs for election again, he has an excellent chance of winning, provided the Democrats don't make significant changes. However, for President Trump to succeed, he must avoid alienating many minority voters and be mindful of his words. While passion is important, blunt words in a sensitive society can be taken negatively and used against the speaker, even if they are speaking from the heart, the old American way.

Our leaders should demonstrate more sportsmanship and integrity. They should understand their people better and recognize the power of game-changing technologies and methodologies.

Common sense would say Hillary had a disconnect with Trump's base, and Trump had a disconnect with a large minority base and changing demographics. Both Trump supporters and Hillary supporters want a better life, law, order, justice, peace, employment, security, safety, and affordable healthcare. We should have faith in our Constitution, agencies, judiciary, and intelligence. They should be held accountable if they fail to catch any cheating.

A Call for Common Sense in Democracy

Instead of showing up once or twice every four years or for a town hall meeting just to make promises, our leaders need to understand that the problems persist and often worsen. Our democratic system is turning into an entertainment spectacle for the world. Rather than understanding real issues, we focus on ratings, speculations, and the opinions of political pundits instead of the people who actually elect officials.

What Have We Done to Our System? First, we focus on ratings and speculations instead of facts. Media experts then make things spicier to generate more money, which creates more polarization, division, panic, fear, and hate. Instead of addressing real issues objectively, our leaders and populace look at media numbers influenced by investors, lobbyists, and corporations.

National Interest vs. Personal Gain: It seems our ego, desires for dominance, and personal profit motives often supersede national interests. Some media gurus twist national interest logic into socialism, but this isn't about becoming a monk or implementing high taxes and restrictions like socialism. It's about using common sense and focusing on positive change.

The Problem with Twisting Words: Twisting words, creating fear and hype, and turning thought-provoking positive ideas into negative propaganda is becoming a significant issue. We need to focus on common sense and our people. Instead of listening to high-profile consultants and political gurus influenced by corporations and lobbyists, we should pay attention to the real issues affecting Americans. We often get so caught up in technology, numbers, and winning that we lose connection with our own people.

Bridging the Divide: A New Approach to Democracy: In a democracy, if the incumbent wins with 51% to 49%, what good does that do for the 49%? This narrow margin highlights and perpetuates existing polarization. How can we prevent this divide from growing wider?

Imagine if 100% of the Population Voted: The results might not be so close, and the true voice of the people would be better represented. But let's explore another viable solution that could transform this 51-49% divide into a strength, bolstering democracy and the American spirit.

A Council Setting: Representing All the People: Instead of having a winner-takes-all approach, why not adopt a council setting where both candidates play significant roles? For instance, in a 51-49% election, the candidate with 51% becomes President, and the candidate with 49% becomes Vice President or part of a governing council that includes the 49% leader too. This structure, inspired by the Muslim Shura council system, ensures that competent, qualified leaders from the populace are part of a council that represents all the people, not just the majority. Note: In reality, we are a Republic and don't practice true democracy, but we should. We should only preach democracy and democratic values to others when we practice true democracy ourselves.

Benefits of Collaborative Leadership

1. **Unified Representation:** Both leaders work together, representing the entire population, reducing feelings of alienation among minority voters.
2. **Balanced Governance:** Policies and decisions would reflect a broader spectrum of views, leading to more balanced and inclusive governance.
3. **Reduced Polarization:** Collaboration fosters a spirit of cooperation and compromise, diminishing the partisan divide.
4. **Strengthened Democracy:** Ensuring nearly half the population still has a strong voice in leadership reinforces democratic principles and promotes unity.

Avoiding the Point of No Return: Without such measures, the nation risks becoming increasingly polarized, potentially reaching a point of no return. This innovative approach to democracy could be the key to preventing that scenario, fostering a more harmonious and effective government.

Conclusion: It's time to rethink how we handle election results in our democracy. By implementing a council setting where both major candidates share power, we can bridge the divide, represent all citizens, and strengthen our democratic foundations. This is not just about winning elections; it's about ensuring a united, prosperous future for all Americans.

Should Global Peace Supersede Short-Term National Interests? Are We Truly Committed to Global Peace?

Reading the news these days can be confusing. On one hand, we aspire for nations like Azerbaijan and Armenia to live peacefully and work together. However, these two nations seem to harbor intense animosity towards each other, possibly even more than India and Pakistan. Despite this, our policymakers aim to become peacemakers and foster friendship between eternal enemies like Azerbaijan and Armenia, and Pakistan and India. Yet, when it comes to collaborating with China and Russia, there is noticeable reluctance.

A Double Standard in Policy? Americans don't share the same deep-rooted animosity towards China and Russia that exists between Armenia and Azerbaijan or between India and Pakistan. However, our traditional intelligence and policy mindset insists on countering perceived rivals at any cost, often exaggerating these rivalries. This contradictory stance raises questions about our sincerity towards global peace.

The Space Economics Perspective: The Space Economics article in this book delves into this mindset, proposing a new approach with practical solutions. It suggests that policymakers and leaders who cling to insecurities, lack competence, and adopt a 'warmonger attitude' are likely to fear genuine peace and collaboration. A 'warmonger attitude' refers to a belligerent or aggressive approach to international relations, often prioritizing military solutions over diplomatic ones. This mindset, the article argues, is a barrier to achieving global peace and collaboration.

Moving Towards a Visionary Approach: Imagine a world where our US State Department's efforts are wholeheartedly dedicated, and our top policymakers demonstrate to the world that American diplomats and leaders are committed to fostering peace between staunch enemies like Israel and Palestine, Azerbaijan and Armenia, and India and Pakistan. In such a world, where we encourage arch-rivals to collaborate peacefully and practice what we preach, collaboration with China and Russia is not only possible but can be actively pursued, and it is imperative to lead by example.

This visionary approach can lead to a more stable and prosperous global community, reducing tensions, promoting innovation, and building trust among nations. Let's commit to making this vision a reality and demonstrate that American leadership is rooted in a genuine commitment to global peace and cooperation.

A World Beyond Short-Term Interests: We can create a future that embodies our highest ideals by prioritizing long-term global peace over short-term national interests. Adopting this visionary approach will:

1. **Foster Global Stability:** True collaboration and peaceful coexistence lead to a more stable and prosperous world, where conflicts are minimized, and economies thrive.
2. **Reduce Tensions:** Proactive engagement with perceived rivals can significantly diminish unnecessary tensions and conflicts, paving the way for more harmonious international relations.
3. **Promote Innovation:** Global collaboration encourages technological and economic advancements, benefiting all nations and driving progress in unprecedented ways.
4. **Build Trust:** Genuine efforts towards peace build trust and strengthen diplomatic ties, creating a foundation for lasting international cooperation.

The Call to Action: It's time for US policymakers to rise to the challenge and lead by example. Let's demonstrate our commitment to peace not just in words, but through bold, visionary actions. These actions can transform the world and secure a brighter, more unified future for all. Let us move beyond rhetoric and take concrete steps toward a world where our shared humanity triumphs over divisions.

Together, we can achieve global peace and prosperity, proving that America's leadership is grounded in wisdom, courage, and an unwavering commitment to a better world.

Conclusion: It's crucial that we rethink our approach to global peace and national interests. By prioritizing sincere and visionary collaboration over short-term gains, we can work towards a more peaceful and united world. Let's strive for a future where our actions reflect our global peace and cooperation ideals, not just strategic interests. When one collaborates and creates synergy, strategic interests automatically come into play; this is a call to action, and we all can play a role in it.

Was the Russia-Ukraine Conflict Avoidable?

The Russia-Ukraine conflict was a devastating event that might have been avoided by implementing forward-thinking ideas, like those discussed in the Space Economics section of this book. Tulsi Gabbard, a respected voice I admire greatly, warned of the impending conflict and suggested ways to prevent it. Unfortunately, her insights were overlooked, possibly due to the agendas of policymakers and planners on both sides.

The Cost of War: We must remember that in war, the first casualty is truth. War and aggression are fundamentally wrong, regardless of the circumstances. Russia felt threatened by NATO's realignment, especially the prospect of Ukraine joining NATO. The U.S. and its allies were aware of Putin's likely reaction, yet both sides remained stubborn. Imagine if Russia or China had their own treaty organizations, and Mexico or Canada wanted to join them, threatening NATO allies. Would the U.S. have acted differently? I think the U.S. would have bombed the shit out of Mexico or Canada. This scenario suggests that American policymakers could have offered alternative solutions to Russia and Ukraine to avoid the chaos.

However, some policymakers wanted to play a grand chessboard for supremacy and world dominance. Did they achieve any world dominance from the chaos in Afghanistan, Iraq, Syria, or Libya? Those who created that chaos only fueled anti-American sentiments in those regions and around the world, benefiting nothing except the corporations that made weapons and the rivals who wanted those countries in ruins.

The American public should ask policymakers what benefits everyday Americans gained from these wars. These actions made the world more dangerous, created more refugees (many of whom ended up coming to the U.S. on the American taxpayer's tab), and reduced beautiful places to rubble. There was no value placed on human life—neither theirs nor our soldiers'—as we sent our soldiers into harm's way, affecting families here in the U.S. and in those regions.

Why don't those corporations read my Space Economics article and put their energies into something more profitable and futuristic where they can earn respect, too?

The American public should demand that any war-propagating senators and policymakers first send their own sons and daughters to war if they are so patriotic. That would prove their patriotism.

The Role of Social Media: These incidents often lead to confusion and the rise of conspiracy theories fueled by social media. Hypothetical narratives on social media can be convincing and deepen the rift between East and West. For instance, some argue that the U.S. waged war on Iraq and Libya for Petro-Dollar reasons and that if the U.S. can conduct pre-emptive strikes for security reasons, why is Russia different? Similarly, if Israel can attack Iraq's nuclear plant in 1981 for security reasons, why can't Russia do the same? These arguments circulate widely and exacerbate tensions.

Provocation and Accountability: When the U.S. and its allies knew that pushing for Ukraine's NATO membership would provoke Russia, why did they continue? A good lawyer might argue that if Russia is guilty, the repeated media frenzy and the U.S. encouraging Ukraine to join NATO could be seen as contributing to the conflict.

A Vision for the Future: Imagine a world where superpowers stop spending resources on countering each other's negative actions and ideologies and instead focus on building their own strengths. This approach would lead to greater progress and stability. The

Space Economics section in this book offers recommendations for achieving this vision.

Conclusion: The Russia-Ukraine conflict highlights the need for visionary leadership and proactive diplomacy. By adopting a more collaborative and less confrontational approach, we can work towards a future where such devastating conflicts are avoided. Let's learn from this and strive for a world where peace and cooperation are prioritized over short-term national interests.

What About Taiwan?

Let's talk about Taiwan. If some of you remember, Nancy Pelosi's intentional visit to Taiwan provoked China. Why not fix the U.S. problems before considering those of other countries? Taiwanese are not U.S. taxpayers; Americans are. Some say Taiwan is a sovereign state bullied by China, so we need to take the side of the weak because we have high moral ground and do business with Taiwan. If we genuinely have high moral ground and believe Taiwan is a sovereign state, then Nancy, why didn't you visit the sovereign state of Palestine, too? Moreover, we do more business with China than with Taiwan. So, your logic doesn't hold up.

Imagine this scenario: in the future, Alaska declares independence and wants to do business with Russia, OR Texas declares independence or starts a secession movement, and the Chinese President decides to visit Texas to give them additional moral support because Texas provides some cattle to China. Would the mainland of the U.S. be happy about it? What would we do then?

The Bigger Picture: Our focus should be on solving our own problems before meddling in others'. The American public deserves our attention and resources more than any foreign issue. By prioritizing our taxpayers, our economy, and our stability, we can build a stronger, more resilient nation.

A Call for Consistency: If we truly stand for moral principles, we must apply them consistently. Otherwise, our actions appear hypocritical and self-serving. By addressing our internal issues first and maintaining a consistent foreign policy, we can truly uphold the values we claim to represent.

Conclusion: It's time for American policymakers to focus on the home front. Our taxpayers deserve it, our economy needs it, and our global credibility depends on it. Let's put America first and ensure that our actions abroad are consistent with our values at home.

Is Illegal Immigration a Problem, or Did We Make It THE PROBLEM?

Legal Immigration: A Boon for the Nation

Legal immigration is not a problem. In fact, it attracts skilled and qualified individuals and investors who contribute significantly to the economy. These immigrants bring exceptional capabilities, knowledge, wealth, unique perspectives, and diversity, benefiting organizations and society. Legal immigrants must meet stringent requirements to become U.S. citizens, including proving continuous residence for a specific number of years, maintaining employment, demonstrating good character, providing tax records, and maintaining a clean record. These criteria are often more demanding than what some U.S.-born citizens might fulfill.

For instance, even a foreigner working for the U.S. Embassy abroad typically needs 15 to 20 years of service with a clean record to be eligible for a Green Card, followed by another five years to become a U.S. citizen. Is it fair to those hardworking, honest, clean-record U.S. Embassy employees working tirelessly for 15 to 20 years for a Green Card while illegals can cross the border and bypass all the rules and laws?

When I mentioned this to one of my friends, he said, "Asif, it can be a ticking time-bomb. Looking at the U.S. sue culture, U.S. Embassy employees waiting for years may get the services of a brilliant U.S. law firm, who may cash in on this opportunity by suing the U.S. government, policymakers, and individuals who do not stop illegal immigration. This seems like discrimination and racism because illegals get a pass by bypassing all the checks that Embassy employees go through to get U.S. residency. In fact, a brilliant lawyer may even prove that this is because of incompetence or special treatment to illegals."

If the law were properly enforced, would caravans of illegal immigrants keep coming? Some argue for humanity and compassion over the law, neglecting that law and order protect humankind. Coming to this country the proper and legal way, standing in line like millions who have done so, is necessary. Turning a blind eye to illegal immigration penalizes and discriminates against those who follow the proper process and patiently wait to join this great nation. Our policymakers should make the system more transparent and timelier for those who want to come the proper way and contribute positively to this nation's development.

We must demand fairness and accountability to protect the integrity of our immigration system and honor the efforts of those who play by the rules. It's time for a change that upholds the values of hard work, dedication, and the American dream for all who seek it the right way.

Illegal Immigration: The Real Issue

Illegal immigration, refugees, and undocumented immigrants present a different scenario. The fundamental problem lies not in immigration itself but in the lack of enforcement of existing laws.

Why do some liberals and Democrats struggle with the simple logic of following the law and waiting for their turn? The issue is implementing the law, not the legal migration process.

1. **Job Availability**: If greedy businesses and culprits do not hire illegal immigrants to save money, will they still come? If American citizens are willing to do the odd and dirty jobs that many illegal immigrants take on, will they still come?

2. **Personal Interests vs. National Interest**: Those who support or help illegal immigrants often do so based on personal emotions and interests. They might want to help friends or relatives or have other personal reasons. However, this way of thinking places personal interests above the law and national interest. A patriot should uphold the law of the land and follow the rules and regulations to ensure the system's integrity and favor the national interest.

Trump's Stand on Illegal Immigration

When President Trump highlighted this sensitive issue, he was labeled a racist and a narcissist by some Democrats and many immigrants. However, enforcing the law is not an act of racism or narcissism. Consider countries like the UAE, China, Saudi Arabia, and Qatar—what would happen to their institutions and legal departments if illegal immigrants started working there in large numbers? In the U.S., a country of immigrants, we have turned a straightforward issue into a complex problem, creating unnecessary division where common sense should prevail.

What Everyone Hears

1. **The Perception of Hate and Fear:** There is a prevailing perception that many of President Trump's supporters treat legal immigrants, especially non-whites, as illegals, creating an environment of hate and fear. Is this in line with Great Christian values? We must ask ourselves if such attitudes reflect the teachings of love, acceptance, and compassion.
2. **The Job Market Reality:** Many hard-working Americans believe immigrants are taking their jobs. In reality, U.S. businesses request H1B visas to meet organizational needs. We face shortages in IT, healthcare, and other fields. Why aren't more Americans entering these professions? Why do corporations seek foreign workers to save money if

Americans are available? Where is the patriotism in this kind of profiteering? There should be a limit to such practices.

3. **Fairness to Legal Immigrants:** Some extreme left Democrats want to legalize undocumented immigrants, rewarding them the same way as law-abiding immigrants who follow the law and wait their turn. Is this fair to those who abide by the rules? Legal immigrants undergo rigorous processes and deserve recognition for their patience and compliance.

4. **Religious Humanitarianism:** Some religious humanitarians say it's God's land and everyone should be allowed. Yes, it is God's land, but God also teaches us to protect our land. If undocumented immigrants have faith, they should follow legal processes and have patience. Religious supporters should volunteer in the countries where immigrants are fleeing and challenge corrupt leaders to fix economic and social injustices. They should also push for the U.S. and the West to seize corrupt leaders' bank accounts as a processing fee for repatriating illegal immigrants. Do we have the courage to address the problem at its source?

5. **Survival of Illegal Immigrants:** How do undocumented immigrants survive in the U.S.? How do they get jobs? Are we responsible for employing them? Are we equally guilty of breaking the law by hiring them? These are questions that need honest answers.

6. **Profiting from War:** Some elites and kingmakers believe war is more profitable than peace. Greed, war, and power conflicts are primary reasons for migration crises. If powers and profiteers didn't provoke wars and fix their own countries, there would be no caravans of refugees or illegal migration. The first casualty of war is truth. Civilian and soldier casualties are often overlooked, as are the long-term efforts to rebuild destroyed cities. War-mongers and leaders should consider the actual costs of conflict. We must ask if we are even looking at the problem correctly.

7. **Misplaced Priorities:** Instead of enforcing the law and addressing root causes, some Americans defending undocumented immigrants seem willing to spend taxpayer money on processing and healthcare for them. Taxpaying U.S. citizens' healthcare isn't free, so why should it be for illegal immigrants? This raises questions about fairness and priorities.

8. **Catch and Release Policy:** Authorities often catch and release undocumented immigrants. This is akin to catching someone breaking the law and releasing them without consequences. Do U.S. police catch and release Americans who violate the law without bail or repercussions? Have we lost common sense?

Conclusion: The discourse on immigration needs to be grounded in common sense, fairness, and adherence to the law. By addressing root causes and maintaining a fair and consistent approach, we can ensure that our policies reflect the values and principles that America stands for. It's time for a balanced perspective that prioritizes national interest while maintaining compassion and justice.

Why Does Nobody Ask the Right Questions?

1. **The Misguided Narrative:** In an interview, Polish leader Dominik Tarczyński boasted about banning Muslim immigration and refugees from Poland, implying Muslims are eager to migrate there and are viewed as undesirables by the Polish majority. But why, before the 1980s, did people from Muslim countries not seek to migrate like nowadays? Wars and foreign interference have caused this shift. We must ask why these wars were waged, who was behind them, and why the financiers and elites behind the scenes always escape accountability while the poor suffer the consequences.

2. **Double Standards**: Saudi Arabia is a Muslim country with minimal crime, yet many Western nations eagerly do business with it and other Middle Eastern countries. If Poland truly despises Muslims, why engage in trade with them? If the Polish truly hate Muslims, why don't Muslim countries impose a no-fly, no-travel list for people like Dominik?

3. **Hypocrisy in Ethics and Humanity**: Why do Western powers, the supposed champions of ethics and humanity, not initiate information campaigns to raise awareness against corrupt leaders in other countries? These campaigns could help fix those countries and provide their people with basic necessities, preventing them from fleeing. It seems that some shortsighted planners and elites want these nations weak to control them easily and allow corrupt leaders to bring their ill-gotten gains into the banks of the "Free World." This hypocrisy shouldn't be mistaken for diplomacy; it's a shortsighted and selfish approach. We are neglecting the fact that the poor and unskilled populace from these nations will flee wherever they get a hint of better life prospects. On the contrary, don't you think that the corrupt elites bringing their corrupt money to law-abiding Western countries won't bring their corruption and tactics to countries where they would bring their money?

4. **The Consequences of Greed**: Elites and kingmakers often find war more profitable than peace, because their vision is limited to that short-term profit-making foresight. Peace, collaboration, and the Space Economics project mentioned in this book have more potential than the profit-making from wars. Greed, war, and power conflicts create waves of refugees and illegal migration. War's first casualty is truth, followed by countless civilian and soldier lives. Rebuilding destroyed cities takes immense time and resources that could have been used to improve economies and lives. Just imagine—it's so easy to bomb and destroy one bridge in seconds, but one forgets that the same bridge needs months, if not years, to rebuild. The warmongers should calculate the true cost of their actions.

5. **The Real Issue**: Instead of addressing the root causes of illegal immigration, some Americans defend it, willing to spend taxpayer money on processing and healthcare for illegal immigrants. U.S. citizens' healthcare isn't free, so why should it be for illegal immigrants? This misplacement of priorities needs to be addressed.

6. **Enforcing the Law**: Authorities often catch and release illegal immigrants, which is akin to catching someone breaking the law and releasing them without consequences. Do U.S. police release American lawbreakers without bail or repercussions? We need to enforce the law consistently. Someday some smart American felons may sue the U.S. government and law enforcement for catching and releasing those illegal immigrants as they got away even with breaking the law; this is discrimination and racism towards our own American citizens prosecuted and jailed.

7. **Personal Accountability**: The mother of a fallen veteran once asked me why politicians don't send their own loved ones to war if they are so committed to national interests. If pro-war decision-makers are unwilling to do this, the public should ask why the poor men's kids' blood is considered cheaper than others.

8. **Lack of Practical Measures by Policymakers**: Why are the corrupt governments' officials from where the illegals and refugees are coming not dealt with like economic terrorists? Bank accounts and businesses of corrupt leaders are swelling in some Western countries; if America and European powers confront those power elites and drug lords with sincere and practical measures, then the economic refugees and illegals from many countries will stop. Some people ask why Financial Action Task Force (FATF) rules don't apply uniformly and transparently to all the countries and politicians. Sometimes it seems that some of the Western banks where some influential corrupt people deposit money are exempt from the FATF rules. On the other hand, some corrupt governments and

selfish leaders milked America like a cow and built their estates and bank accounts. Corrupt leaders are like menaces; they have no loyalty, no religion, no values, or ethics. They are FAKE and a curse to humanity. Unfortunately, most affected countries are Muslim countries; if wars are stopped, Muslim refugees will stop coming. So, our citizens, who don't want refugees, especially many Trump supporters, must show the planners and kingmakers that the power of collaboration, rule of law with strict enforcement, and the profits of peace are far greater than the wars.

9. **Don't Impose Your Way of Life**: Don't impose your way of life and democracy on these countries like Afghanistan and Iraq, Syria, Libya, etc. They will progress through their own learning curve through their own cultural perceptions. As a reaction, imposing our ways mostly ends up in conflict and wars, generating refugees and creating more terrorists. When these refugees come to the West, the simple-minded populace in the West thinks that these refugees and migrants are imposing their way of life on the West. In reality, we tried to impose our way of life on them, which backfired. "Every nation for itself, and God for us all," Lord Canning.

10. **Muslims Should Fix Their Countries**: Many Far-Right leaders in Western countries think and perceive Muslims as negative and evil. If some Western policymakers complain about some Muslim countries' mosques and syllabi talking about the West as conspirers against them and labeling some non-Muslims as impure and infidels, then some Western schools and churches should also not spread stereotyping against Islam and Muslims as evil too. The hate propaganda on both sides is done openly, but no one has the guts to confront the propaganda with the facts and set the record straight. Muslim countries' widely held perception is that most of their corrupt leaders are in cahoots with those responsible for the root cause of these problems, i.e., most of the WEST. Did anyone think why they think like that?

35

11. **Perception Shifts Through Propaganda**: Over the years, through regular propaganda, perceptions have been changed by propagating the wrong concept, i.e., from the clash of civilizations to the war of religions to the conflict of races, and Black Lives Matter. Now, some propagate the perception of the survival of the white race. This narrative only fuels division and strife. The issue started because some policymakers and profiteers promoted the clash of civilization concept to create a market niche in a stealth way to mold a populace to a specific way of life for their own benefits or due to their insecurities, but it backfired eventually. The world will realize one day that it was never the clash of civilizations. Because in the dark ages, the same Muslim society, perceived as backward and a threat now, gave Europe the knowledge to develop; of course, Muslims developed their skills and knowledge further from Greeks and earlier civilizations. It may be a clash between the modern and progressive way of life with the old-thought and rigid ways. So instead of putting each other down and focusing on the differences, focusing on peace and collaboration can take us much farther.

12. **The Fallout of Wars and Interference**: Wars and poking noses into other countries' businesses had a reaction. Not speaking up against corruption at the right time made many countries a mess. Nobody openly asks why the wars were waged, and mostly the Muslim populace were the victims; who is behind the scenes?

Conclusion: The discourse on immigration, war, and international relations needs to be grounded in common sense, fairness, and adherence to the law. By addressing root causes and maintaining a fair and consistent approach, we can ensure that our policies reflect the values and principles that America stands for. It's time for a balanced perspective that prioritizes national interest while maintaining compassion and justice. Let's focus on peace and collaboration instead of perpetuating division and conflict.

Sensitivity and Common Sense: Balancing Respect and Open Dialogue

I understand the need for sensitivity and respect in our interactions, but sometimes it feels like we've taken it too far. In a country that values freedom of speech, it seems increasingly difficult to speak openly about important topics. This is one reason President Trump gained popularity—he speaks common sense to average Americans, addressing issues that people feel but are often too afraid to voice.

I was surprised when I was told that using the phrase "blindly follow" might be sensitive to some people. Similarly, saying "illegal" has become offensive, and the term "illegal immigrant" has been replaced with "undocumented migrant." But why this over-sensitivity? To me, it feels like calling an illegal immigrant an undocumented migrant implies they came legally but just forgot their papers at home. Is that really the case?

If we become too sensitive, the world will eat us alive. Let's use common sense and not change the American personality completely. We should strive for a balance where we can maintain respect and civility without losing our ability to speak frankly and honestly.

What About the Wall?

Why couldn't we build a wall as President Trump promised? Would the wall have been effective? The wall might have helped a little in enhancing security and stopping some of the flow of illegal immigrants, but it wouldn't be a perfect solution. And why was the wall so expensive to build?

President Trump asked for $5.7 billion to complete fencing on the Mexican border (1,900 kilometers only) and even shut down the government to get this approved. Are we not giving too much to the contractors and profiteers? Pakistan completed 2,600 kilometers of a barbed fence wall for $550 million, and we needed a wall for 1,900 kilometers for $5.7 billion; something is not right there. Why not have the American Armed Forces oversee the wall building instead of awarding considerable sums to contractors? If soldiers can build camps, bases, and facilities, why not a wall? Maybe contractors have connections with those who would like to make that wall? The wall doesn't have to be made of bricks; it can be a three-section barbed wire with laser, electricity (from solar), and motion detectors installed every kilometer with national guards supporting the immigration force ICE. Many Pakistani soldiers built 2,600 kilometers of barbed wire wall and sealed the border; many were also killed while completing the task in record time at a fraction of the cost at one of the world's most dangerous borders.

Are we at war with Mexico?

Is our border more hazardous than the Pakistan-Afghan border?

Can't we collaborate with the Mexican government to build something like that at a much lower cost?

Is Pakistani will, spirit, and creativity better than American? I don't think so; our ego, self-interest, and party lines seem to supersede our national interests. We are not united; we have more talent, resources, and capabilities than the rest of the world, but our common-sense seems polluted.

If President Trump supporters are adamant about the wall, why don't they willingly pay a 10% additional tax every year for making the wall for the next five years?

Suppose those on the far left are so committed to supporting illegal immigrants and refugees. Why don't they willingly pay a 10% additional tax each year to cover the necessities for these individuals while their cases are being processed?

The question isn't just about the wall but our priorities, unity, and willingness to put national interests above partisan bickering. It's about finding practical, cost-effective solutions and ensuring our actions reflect our values. Let's use our resources wisely, collaborate with our neighbors, and focus on what truly makes America strong: our spirit of innovation, our commitment to justice, and our dedication to working together for the common good.

Why Nothing Changes: Electing the Same People for the Same Problems!

The only way to approach a problem differently is to change the people involved, who could not get the job done yet. It's time to confront a harsh reality: nothing changes because we keep choosing the same people to address the same problems. We consistently vote for the same politicians who appoint the same diplomats and bureaucrats, expecting different results. But real change requires fresh perspectives and bold leadership. What we are doing now is practicing Einstein's theory of insanity.

Leadership with Vision

Effective leaders possess courage, resilience, risk stamina, and vision. They are brave enough to face challenges head-on, acknowledge their team's contributions, and push beyond conventional boundaries. On the other hand, those who fear their own shadows, lack vision, and avoid risks are unfit for leadership roles. Leaders who are more concerned with presenting a rosy picture to their superiors rather than addressing ground realities undermine progress and innovation.

The Leadership Paradox

People who cannot think beyond the paygrade psyche, scared to take even calculated risks, and in the habit of giving a rosy picture to their bosses, thinking of shortcuts and easy ways out, should not be in positions of authority. This paradox reminds me of a leadership matrix where hardworking and intelligent leaders who sometimes develop insecurities promote dumb and hardworking proteges or prefer their friends, relatives, and ethnicities. Then, the dumb and hardworking promote the lazy and dumb proteges.

Another dilemma is promoting and selecting the ones who are not perceived as a threat and are not that competent. Because some people in high positions don't want to hire people smarter than them, they think of those intelligent people as a threat; this is a defeated and loser psyche, which affects and corrupts the competence and the genesis blocks of the organization. If I were a commander or the CEO loyal to the organization, I would want more intelligent and competent people working with me to gain a competitive advantage and take the organization to the next level. People who are not bold enough to tell the ground realities to the top, and who are reluctant to fix the issues, don't deserve to be in positions of responsibility. A kiss-ass, a fake, or just a photo-op person won't make a long-lasting difference or real impact in getting things done. It may even be counterproductive when it comes to productivity, strengthening institutions, and assisting the top leadership in crisis when the administration and organization need it the most.

A true leader, dedicated to the organization's success, would seek out the most intelligent and capable individuals to foster a competitive edge.

Term and Age Limits

To further ensure dynamic and effective leadership, there should be an age limit for positions such as President, Vice President, Judges, and Senators. Additionally, implementing term limits for Senators would prevent the entrenchment of power and encourage fresh ideas and perspectives. These measures would help mitigate the stagnation caused by long-term incumbency and promote a more responsive and adaptive government.

Diversity and Competence

Despite widespread rhetoric about diversity, inclusion, and equal opportunity, personal biases often prevail in hiring decisions. Friends hire friends, ethnic groups favor their own, and job descriptions are tailored to fit pre-selected candidates. This practice not only undermines the merit-based system but also hinders the organization's potential for greatness. Also, some individuals misuse the serious issues of racism, discrimination, and minority status as a tactic to deflect from their own incompetency. This approach is neither patriotic nor in the true spirit of American values.

Breaking the Cycle

Joel Osteen's book, *Breakout*, is a valuable resource for those struggling with insecurities in leadership roles. It emphasizes the importance of breaking free from limiting mindsets to achieve extraordinary results. Yet, many organizations continue to overlook qualified prospects due to biases and insecurities, perpetuating a cycle of mediocrity.

The Cost of Short-Sightedness

Hiring based on personal relationships or fulfilling diversity quotas without considering competence is short-sighted. This approach ultimately weakens institutions and, by extension, the nation. In contrast, systems prioritizing talent, hard work, and capabilities, like those seen in competitive economies, are better positioned for sustained success.

Veterans and Competence

I have veteran friends who are people of integrity and high honor. Veterans bring invaluable skills and experiences to the workforce. While honoring their service is important, true meritocracy means allowing veterans to compete based on their abilities without preferential treatment. Veterans, trained to excel under any circumstances, should be confident in their capacity to compete in the broader talent pool.

A Call for Change

It's time for a paradigm shift. We must demand leaders who are not afraid to challenge the status quo, who value competence over convenience, and who foster an environment where the best ideas and talents can thrive. By doing so, we can break the cycle of stagnation and drive meaningful, lasting change. Implementing term and age limits is crucial to ensuring our leaders are capable, dynamic, and forward-thinking, ready to meet the challenges of today and tomorrow.

However, these above-mentioned short-sighted practices will take a toll on the institution and, finally, the nation. So eventually, we are trying our best and persistently bringing down our own system. How long will our system be able to compete with the Chinese socialism-type system where talent, capabilities, and hard work get more precedence?

DIVIDED WE FALL – UNITED WE STAND

Respect for the law and the rule of law should take precedence over political, religious, profiteering, or personal agendas. A troubling phenomenon many Americans hold is that even if a legal immigrant becomes a naturalized citizen, they are never fully perceived as American. Similarly, even when someone is born American but looks Chinese or Indian, they are often seen as foreign. Americans rarely refer to a British, German, or French American as anything other than American, yet this same courtesy is not extended to those of Asian descent. In contrast, countries like Canada more readily embrace their naturalized citizens as true Canadians.

Addressing Illegal Immigration: To solve the issue of illegal immigration and undocumented workers, the government can reduce violations by enforcing the law, timely vetting, and providing work permits to foreign workers genuinely interested in jobs Americans are reluctant to do. American policymakers should consider giving incentives to foreigners through speedy work visas, bringing potential unlawful immigrants into the tax net, ultimately benefiting the government. Those who fail to follow the law should face speedy justice with consequences tied to their native countries. Is this so hard to implement? It's certainly no more complicated than democratizing Afghanistan.

A Vision of Global Unity: Reflecting on the book "World With No Visa," I'm reminded of a quote from its preface: *"This book is a fiction leading to my personal feelings. It is simply a prayer to unite people at the lowest level with the testament to help each other, establish peace everywhere, irrespective of place, religion, and race. Racism is a curse that can only be eliminated through visits, talking to each other about the mutual problems and solving them in the same spirit. It is though a fiction but the quotes are true to the last details. I wanted it to be published in my own simple words with no editing to avoid twisting my personal feelings. This book is for a common man to think and change the world if he can, through his governments that he/she elects and ensure good governance by them."*

"I want the 'World With No Visa' to roam:
Delhi without check,
Beijing with love,
London with a kiss,
Washington with wish,
Moscow to miss,
Ankara, Cairo, and Baghdad to grace.
That is the human race;
That we want to embrace.
Nowhere to wait,
No one to hate.
Sayonara to all,
No atom at all.
Surrender at Mecca and Medina,
Return to Pakistan to live in peace."

—*Rab Nawaz Choudhry, Group Captain (Retd)*

A Call for Self-Improvement: However, our current mindset isn't ready for such openness until we first put our own house in order. Embracing this vision requires us to foster unity, respect for diversity, and a genuine commitment to equality within our borders. Only then can we hope to extend this harmony globally, ensuring a future where divided we fall, but united we stand.

Reciprocity in Immigration and Property Ownership Policies?

In the spirit of fairness, we should re-evaluate our policies regarding immigration, citizenship, and property ownership. Many Americans are unaware of the stark differences between our policies and those of other nations. For instance, in countries like Saudi Arabia and the UAE, even if someone is born there, they cannot obtain citizenship. This contrasts sharply with the U.S., where birthright citizenship is granted regardless of parental nationality.

Citizenship and Birthright: It's well-known that nationals from other countries sometimes bring their pregnant wives to the U.S. specifically to give birth here, thereby securing American citizenship for their child. Should we allow this practice to continue when these same countries do not offer reciprocal opportunities? Shouldn't there be a requirement that at least one parent must be an American citizen for the child to be granted citizenship? This change would ensure that the privilege of U.S. citizenship is not exploited by those who do not extend the same generosity.

Property Ownership: Another issue lies in property ownership. Foreign nationals can easily purchase land in the U.S., often backed by their governments or large companies. This drives up property prices, making it increasingly difficult for American citizens to afford land. Meanwhile, American citizens are often restricted from buying property in these foreign countries. For example, non-residents cannot own land in many countries, including some in the Middle East and

Asia. This lack of reciprocity puts Americans at a disadvantage, both at home and abroad.

A Call for Reciprocity: Most Western countries, including the U.S., are known for their openness to immigration and dual citizenship. People and companies from other nations can invest here with relative ease. However, there should be a principle of reciprocity in place. Why should we allow nationals from countries that do not grant similar privileges to Americans to take advantage of our generous policies?

In some countries getting permanent immigration or citizenship is virtually impossible for foreigners, even if they have lived and worked there for decades. If some countries do not allow other nationals to immigrate, gain citizenship, or own property, should we continue to offer these opportunities to their citizens? And some of those countries are our staunch allies.

Common Sense and Fairness: Critics often complain about the U.S. immigration system being strict or slow, but they rarely consider the policies of other nations, which are far more restrictive. Are we using common sense when we allow this imbalance to persist? Shouldn't there be a fair exchange of rights and privileges between nations?

Conclusion: It's time for a thoughtful reconsideration of our policies. Reciprocity in immigration and property ownership would ensure fairness and protect American interests. We need to ask ourselves: Are we being too generous at our own expense? Shouldn't we demand the same opportunities for our citizens that we provide to others? By implementing a reciprocity clause, we can create a more balanced and fair system for everyone.

Why Do We Insist on Changing Others' Ways of Life and Promoting Our Type of Democracy?

Why are we so determined to change others' ways of life and insist on our type of democracy?

Democracy is a government by the people, for the people, and indeed, it is an excellent form of governance. However, why are we so insistent on altering other systems by claiming there is a threat to our way of life? At times, in our efforts to change others, we end up altering our own way of life.

Why Do We Have Double Standards with Refugees?

During the Ukraine war, some of my Muslim friends pointed out the stark contrast in the West's response to different refugee crises. The Western media more openly embraced Ukrainian refugees and continuously reported on Russian atrocities. However, similar warmth, human rights advocacy, and high moral standards were not as evident for refugees from Africa, Kashmir, Syria, Libya, Palestine, Rohingya, and Iraq.

The West frequently advocates for equality, diversity, and combating racism and discrimination, yet the actions during the Ukraine crisis spoke louder than words, exposing a stark hypocrisy. These observations have led some non-whites and Muslims to feel that the West does not treat all refugees equally. **If this is the case, then please don't be hypocritical and stop claiming "no discrimination based on religion and color."** If we truly stand against discrimination based on religion and color, our actions should consistently reflect those values. However, it is worth noting that during the recent Israel-Hamas conflict, the media coverage did include more reporting on Palestinian civilian casualties and suffering than in previous instances.

WHERE IS OUR COMMON SENSE?

Are We Moving Towards a Civil War?

Instead of focusing on our progress, we are more focused on countering our rivals' negative propaganda and fear of the unknown, often and at a great expense. We are pouring money into security measures, expanding security manuals, and supporting buffer nations around our rivals. If we directed our efforts towards our own progress, other countries wouldn't be able to compete. Yet, our mindset is becoming more paranoid.

We are a nation of faith, and rather than building on our resources and capabilities, we are engaging in preemptive planning to secure resources globally and counter our rivals. While we advocate for collaboration, freedom, creativity, and a free spirit, our actions suggest we are moving towards isolationism and chaos. In trying to surpass China and Russia, our system of "checks and balances" on our own citizens is beginning to resemble theirs.

We have the best constitution in the world, alongside unmatched technological and media power. Ironically, it seems our enemies may be using our own media and constitution against us in a form of hybrid warfare, causing us to turn on each other without even realizing it. We might be naively and enthusiastically aiding our enemies' success through our own actions.

We focus more on concepts like the clash of civilizations, which broadens rifts and fuels conflict, rather than working on collaboration and commonalities. In his article "Is America Heading for Civil War?" Edward Luce discusses the widening rift between small white towns and big cities, and how many feel justified in using violence to achieve their political ends.

Where are we heading, and are we using any common sense?

Are We Confusing and Compromising Competency with Diversity?

Diversity and inclusiveness are blessings when appropriately utilized. They bring different perspectives and synergy to an organization. However, competency should not be confused or compromised with diversity. Education should be skills and proficiency-based, as well as morally and human-oriented, not solely money-oriented. If our education system is not focused on skills and proficiency, and our hiring practices are not based on merit and competency but rather on political or personal connections, color, or religious preferences, we risk losing our competitive edge over our rivals.

English as the Official Language

This is the United States of America, and English should be the official and only language for Americans. Making English the official language could help unify the nation and streamline government processes. A common language fosters better communication and understanding among citizens, promoting cultural integration and a shared national identity.

Yes, it's good to learn multiple languages, but that should be a personal preference. Learning languages can increase one's skill set and qualifications. In schools, learning another language should be encouraged at a young age, allowing children to become fluent later in life. However, imposing another specific language on all the populace is not perceived as a learning opportunity but as a threat, and may even create division and animosity.

Official Language Policies in Other Countries: In countries like Germany, France, Sweden, and Norway, immigrants are required to learn the official language to gain citizenship or decent jobs. This policy ensures integration and unity within the country. Should we add options for Chinese and Hindi if we have more Chinese or Indian immigrants?

Streamlined Government: Making English the official language could simplify government operations and reduce translation costs.

Freedom of Speech: Some argue that mandating a single language could infringe upon individuals' freedom of expression. However, this logic doesn't hold up when considering the current American situation. Freedom of speech is about the right to express one's opinions and ideas without fear of government retaliation or censorship. It does not necessitate the use of multiple languages for official and business purposes.

Practicality and Efficiency: In a diverse society, having a common language for official matters ensures clarity, efficiency, and cohesion. It prevents misunderstandings and ensures everyone is on the same page, literally and figuratively. This practical approach does not restrict anyone from speaking their native language in personal or cultural contexts.

Preservation of Cultural Identity: Mandating English for official use does not mean eradicating other languages. Individuals can still speak their native languages at home, within their communities, and in cultural contexts. This policy is about creating a unified framework for public and professional interactions, not about suppressing cultural identities.

Equality and Opportunity: A single official language ensures equal access to information and opportunities. It levels the playing field, allowing all citizens to participate fully in civic life, regardless of their background. This approach promotes inclusivity rather than exclusion.

Precedent and Global Norms: Many countries have official language policies without infringing on freedom of speech. The goal is to foster unity and effective communication, not to limit personal expression. The U.S. can adopt a similar approach, balancing practical needs with respect for individual rights.

Economic and Employment Impact: Requiring proficiency in English for citizenship and jobs could potentially improve economic opportunities for all residents. It ensures that everyone can participate fully in the workforce and reduces language barriers that might hinder business operations. This would allow for smoother interactions and more efficient services across the board.

Cultural Integration: Encouraging the use of English can promote cultural integration and a shared national identity. It can help new immigrants assimilate more easily into American society, creating a more cohesive and harmonious community. It's great if individuals want to learn multiple languages—good for them—but why promote a two-tier language system?

Reducing Frustration Among Citizens: Many hardworking Americans feel frustrated when they perceive that foreign languages are taking precedence over English. Addressing this concern through a unified language policy could alleviate some of these frustrations and foster a greater sense of national unity. This is about fairness and preserving the American way of life.

Referendum for Democratic Decision: Why not have a referendum on this issue, ensuring that 100% of the U.S. citizen populace must vote? This would ensure that the decision reflects the will of the people and provides a democratic solution to this issue, giving everyone a voice in the matter. It's a fair and straightforward way to settle this debate once and for all.

A Shift in Focus: From Rivalry to Progress

Is maligning each other and extensively countering rivals the most effective way?

Currently, when we look at the world's traditional policymakers, it seems that various regional and global rivals—like the U.S., Russia, China, India, Pakistan, Saudi Arabia, Iran, Israel, Armenia, Azerbaijan, and others—spend a lot of energy, resources, and time countering each other. Instead of putting money into rivalry, imagine if nations used their energies, resources, and funds to develop their own people and economies. This approach would be much more productive.

Prioritizing Development Over Rivalry: I am not suggesting that we forget about security and due diligence. The U.S. is already far ahead of its rivals, China and Russia combined, in terms of military, economy, talent, and resources. If most of the resources that the U.S. currently invests in countering its adversaries were redirected towards further developing our nation—whether it be infrastructure, training, R&D, military, agriculture, healthcare, etc.—we would continue to gain momentum that our adversaries could not match.

Focus on Self-Improvement: We should not worry about countering others' negative propaganda or successes; we should focus on our development, people, and achievements. A competent and top student doesn't focus on countering other students' success but on their own studies and success. Similarly, a successful business concentrates on improving its product quality and services. Focusing on countering rivals' products without improving one's own won't lead to long-term success; that's a short-term strategy of the incompetent. Irrefutable success and the increasing gap between the competent and less competent will settle the long-run scores.

Leading by Example: Our focus should be on building our people, infrastructure, and economy, and leading the world into the next industrial revolution, which could be space exploration. Instead of countering rivals, we should strive for peace and collaboration. Imagine if the U.S. and USSR combined their space exploration resources instead of fighting each other—humans might have been on Mars 10 years ago.

The Power of Collaboration: Those who focus on their own success and strive for peace and collaboration will inevitably go far ahead. The world will benefit more from nations working together rather than against each other. We can create a future where progress and peace prevail by prioritizing development and cooperation over rivalry.

By rethinking our approach and focusing on building up our own strengths, we can ensure a more prosperous and harmonious world for everyone.

Why Are We Not Consistent on Human Rights Issues?

We Americans pride ourselves on our high moral standards and our commitment to standing up for human rights. When countries like China, Pakistan, Afghanistan, and Russia violate human rights, we are very vocal. However, our response is often muted when it comes to some of our allies. Our values should be consistent; we must not act like hypocrites.

Consistency and Integrity: I see our top policymakers thinking like Democrat-Americans, Republican-Americans, Israeli-Americans, Armenian-Americans, Indian-Americans, etc., but rarely do I see an American-American stance. For instance, in the March 1 State of the Union address, President Biden mentioned Russian atrocities in Ukraine. We frequently condemn Russian tanks in Ukraine, but where is the same vigor to stand for the oppressed when Israeli tanks or Indian troops commit similar actions?

Addressing Anti-American Sentiment: Our policymakers wonder why ordinary Muslims worldwide have rising anti-American sentiments and don't trust the U.S. Yes, Israel is our staunch ally, and the U.S. will always stand by Israel as a big brother. Still, sometimes, the big brother needs to help the younger brother understand dilemmas that might be hurting both. This includes addressing actions that increase hatred and animosity in many parts of the world.

Guiding Our Allies: Israel has much to offer the world, from technological and medical advancements to agricultural innovations and economic development ideas. Peace and collaboration are the way forward. Sometimes, to avert future disasters, Big Brother needs to guide staunch allies on what they might be overlooking. By doing so, we can strengthen our relationships and improve global perceptions.

Effective Human Rights Advocacy: Our efforts and resources sometimes go to waste when we fail to act consistently. We did a brilliant job raising awareness about Chinese human rights violations against Muslim Uyghurs. However, many Muslims doubted our intentions, viewing it as a strategy to counter China's growing trade and economic influence rather than genuine concern for human rights.

The Need for Genuine Commitment: If we were truly serious about human rights violations, we would apply the same level of awareness campaigns to guide our allies, like India and Israel, to avoid such violations. This would make our efforts against Chinese violations more credible and effective. Consistency in our human rights stance would reinforce our integrity and strengthen our global leadership.

The American-American Stance: By adopting a consistent and principled approach to human rights, we can restore trust and respect worldwide. Our commitment to human rights should not waver based on political alliances. We must stand firm and apply our values universally, ensuring that we truly lead by example. In conclusion, our policymakers should prioritize an American-American stance that aligns with our core values. By doing so, we can foster peace, collaboration, and mutual respect, making a meaningful impact on the global stage.

What Kind of Free Speech Do We Practice, and Where Is Our Common Sense?

When someone creates cartoons of Prophet Muhammad (PBUH) or speaks against Muslims' feelings about him, many in the Western media defend it as free speech. However, when someone expresses a different opinion about the Holocaust, it often becomes a criminal offense. This inconsistency raises questions about the nature of free speech and our common sense.

The Double Standard in Free Speech: The concept of free speech should be applied consistently. While it's important to protect the right to express opinions, it's equally important to recognize the impact of those opinions on different communities. Defending the right to offend Muslims while criminalizing Holocaust denial highlights a troubling double standard.

A Call for Consistency and Sensitivity: When I was writing this, one of my friends cautioned me, saying I might be labeled as anti-Semitic. This surprised me because I am not anti-Semitic; I do not deny the Holocaust. I firmly believe that Hitler's murder of millions of innocent Jews was a horrific atrocity. The Jewish American friends I know are sensible, intelligent, and kind people. True friends should be able to speak honestly and use common sense when discussing sensitive issues.

The Need for Honest Dialogue: Only a good friend dares to tell another when something is wrong. Honest and respectful dialogue is essential in addressing these double standards. By fostering open conversations, we can better understand each other's perspectives and work towards a more consistent and fair approach to free speech.

Moving Forward: To ensure that free speech is genuinely free and fair, we must apply it consistently across all issues. This means protecting speech that may offend one group just as vigorously as we protect speech that may offend another. By doing so, we uphold the true spirit of free speech and demonstrate a commitment to fairness and common sense.

In conclusion, let's strive for a more balanced approach to free speech that respects all perspectives and applies common sense. Only then can we create a society where freedom of expression is truly valued and protected.

How Do We Discourage the Conspiracy Mindset?

I often hear from some of my Muslim friends and Muslims from other countries that Israel and America are conspiring against Muslims, and that the CIA doesn't want Muslims to succeed. Instead of focusing on development, fixing problems like corruption, and promoting peace and collaboration, it's easier to find excuses and blame others.

The Conspiracy Dilemma: A friend of mine from Pakistan illustrated this mindset perfectly with an interesting scenario: "A Pakistani raised in Pakistan always looked for conspiracy theories and believed there was a building in the West where powerbrokers conspired to destroy countries like Pakistan. However, when this same Pakistani goes to the West to study, he realizes there is no such building. In fact, the building is in Pakistan, where Pakistanis are conspiring against themselves to bring down their own country."

An Interesting Example: Once, I was visiting Pakistan during a time of severe floods and witnessed the destruction they caused. I was taken aback by a comment from a very educated man who said, "This is the wrath of God." Curious, I asked him how he knew this. He answered, "Because of the immorality and adoption of vulgar Western values, and some Pakistani government officials unconditionally supporting the U.S." I was even more surprised by his explanation, but I offered my perspective. I suggested that it could be the other way around: maybe God the Almighty Allah was providing millions of gallons of water to address water shortages, generate electricity, and improve irrigation. In my mind, it was a blessing from God the Almighty Allah. However, I pointed out that the government and officials were not ready for it because they had not planned accordingly to harness and store that blessing.

Education as a Refutation Tool: This kind of mindset and rival propaganda can be refuted through education. Half of the world's politicians and leaders are quick to blame the U.S. for their problems, attempting to hide their own incompetencies. When one is a superpower, many jealous rivals try to malign you. Instead of blaming others, these leaders should focus on solving their problems with the resources God has given them.

Changing Perspectives Through Actions: To combat this conspiracy mindset, actions speak louder than words. For example, when someone disrespects Prophet Muhammad, if countries like Israel were the first to condemn it and pass laws against such free speech, it might make many educated Muslim youths reconsider their beliefs and move away from conspiracy theories.

Promoting Self-Development and Collaboration: Encouraging self-development and collaboration within Muslim communities is crucial. By focusing on education, economic growth, and fighting corruption, Muslims can build stronger, more resilient societies. This proactive approach diminishes the allure of conspiracy theories and empowers individuals to take control of their own destinies.

Building Trust Through Positive Examples: Positive actions and genuine support from nations often perceived as adversaries can help build trust and reduce conspiracy thinking. When countries demonstrate respect and solidarity in times of crisis or controversy, it can lead to a reevaluation of long-held beliefs and foster a more cooperative global environment.

Conclusion: To discourage the conspiracy mindset, we must promote education, self-improvement, and collaboration. Additionally, nations should strive to build trust through positive actions and genuine support. By focusing on these strategies, we can help individuals move beyond baseless theories and work towards a more understanding and united world.

Do We Need to Re-visit Our Foreign Policy Strategy and Thinking?

Before answering this question, we should ask first: as peacemakers and nation-builders, did we create more chaos? If we caused more turmoil and hate toward America, then we must analyze ourselves critically.

Focus on Domestic Issues: We are so engaged in fixing other countries' problems that we sometimes don't realize what's happening at home. We should spend on our own and make the U.S. much better and far ahead; our success and advancement would be a lesson to those who oppose us and don't believe in our values.

Rising Anti-American Sentiment: Let's look at Iraq, Afghanistan, Syria, Pakistan, etc.; is there an increasing anti-American sentiment at the populace level in those regions?

Missteps in Afghanistan: In Afghanistan, we supported those leaders who needed a very high number of bodyguards themselves to roam around in their own homeland. In contrast, the Taliban seemed to walk around more carefree than those we were supporting. I don't know how far it is true, but one of my friends mentioned that we had governors who feared for their lives going to their own provinces. We were spending money on activities like posting posters for women's rights around the city, neglecting that many women didn't know how to read. Have we gone too far propagating freedom and women's rights and enforcing our way of life on others that we don't even know what we are doing? I don't understand how one could rely on those natives stabilizing Afghanistan whose own properties and bank accounts were in the U.S., Switzerland, and countries worldwide. I was surprised to hear a comment from a veteran that some Afghan elites helping the U.S. had in mind to leave Afghanistan as soon as they get an opportunity or visa for themselves and their families to settle in Western countries like the U.S., U.K., Australia, etc. Usually, they had this kind of five-year plan in their mind from the first day of work. I don't know how far that is correct, but if it has even some shreds of truth, how did we expect the situation would stabilize when the people hired to stabilize the situation themselves were looking to flee to the Western world? Did any policymaker or analyst look into actual ground realities? Sometimes, it seems, nobody wanted to make any drastic changes on their watch because change could have been riskier or backfired. Or was it the hybrid of corporate profiteering, bureaucratic egoism, and political-ideological-regional partisan at its climax, or was just the common sense missing? We spent so much money on Afghanistan; it looks like everyone was milking America like a cow, but at whose expense, the U.S. taxpayers' expense. We would have benefited more if we could have spent so much money on building spaceships and colonizing Mars; we might have hired many Afghans to develop a colony on Mars.

Women's Rights and Cultural Sensitivity: By the way, in propagating women's rights, why didn't we use chapters from the Koran (from Chapter Nisa (Women)) to at least show the Taliban that the Koran has given more rights to women than the Taliban are offering? So, at least give your women rights per the Koran. But I think it would have been a hard pill to swallow for those who don't understand Islam or don't like Islam. So, we are trying to tell Afghans to give their women rights, and we are taking away the rights of our women by overturning abortion laws; that's not a good sign.

Questioning Our Strategy Against the Taliban: On the contrary, we lost to the Taliban despite our well-trained, experienced policymakers, many with Harvard and Yale think tank exposure, with such firepower and an organized military, with abundant resources and agencies like CIA and MI6, and at times, even ISI and RAW supporting the U.S. forces. Taliban didn't have any education and training like our top policymakers, no Harvard-type university foresight, and not even a regular army with weaponry and technology that we Americans had access to. Am I missing something? Were we even using common sense or just making things complicated to ensure victory for our opponents? Do we need these wars? Will a space venture be not more profitable and farsighted, where we would collaborate with fellow humans to go beyond what others couldn't imagine in the history of humankind?

The Iraq Experience: Let's look at Iraq. We liberated Iraq from Saddam Hussein and won, but what was the first thing Paul Bremer did after winning? I don't know if it was the right choice. The traditional intelligence guys have their own intelligence models. So, instead of thinking out of the box using common sense, was it a good idea to dismantle the Iraqi Army or offer them an alternative? How would you feel if you worked hard most of your life, achieved a rank/title, earned a pension, and suddenly a foreigner dismantled you and 400,000 others with a pen stroke? If even 20,000 of those disgruntled, highly trained troops joined ISIS? Just imagine the consequences. What have you done, Mr. Bremer? Alternatively, if the U.S. had integrated those 400,000 troops under the US-Iraq flag and re-instituted their pay and pensions from their own oil money. Then, instead of providing support to ISIS and making Iran stronger, we could have had an auxiliary army supporting the U.S., fighting for the U.S., and winning the minds and hearts of Iraqis by Iraqis. Not to forget, with our actions, we indirectly provided those trained, disgruntled, dismantled army soldiers as a gift to ISIS and bad guys in Iraq, Syria, and other places, and also increased Iranian influence.

Winning Hearts and Minds: The most important thing is winning the hearts and minds and the will to fight. Why do we sometimes seem to choose those whose will to fight seems less than our opponents? Are we missing something here?

The Pakistan Paradox: Let's look at Pakistan, a staunch American ally of America for decades, and the Pakistani public that was pro-American for decades. How beautifully did we turn a pro-American populace against us?

Pakistan's Historical Support: Pakistan was a U.S. ally for more than 40 years; once a member of SEATO and CENTO partnered with the U.S. in the Southeast Asian region, India was a staunch ally of the USSR, and the USSR had a strong influence in the area. Pakistan provided the Peshawar Badaber base to the U.S. to spy on the USSR. After the 1960 U-2 incident and the capture of the American pilot Francis Gary Powers by the Russians, Pakistan was under the direct wrath of the USSR. Pakistan took that bashing and stuck with the U.S. because Pakistan considered the U.S. a good friend. Let's look at some other things: Pakistan helped President Richard Nixon and Henry Kissinger meet with the CCP Chairman Mao Zedong and initiated bilateral relations between the U.S. and China. Pakistan assisted the U.S. in supporting the Afghan Mujahedeen fighting the USSR in the 1980s, eventually leading to the USSR's collapse. In the second Afghan war, Pakistan assisted the U.S. again, sacrificing more than 70,000 people, including 30,000 Pakistan Army soldiers, and more than 150 billion dollars of economic losses. Here, I can keep going with the list of many small events, such as in 1992, the Pakistan Army, with the U.N. peacekeeping, played a vital role in rescuing U.S. Army Rangers and Delta Force in Mogadishu, Somalia, during the operation "RESTORE HOPE." So, what went wrong? The U.S. provided a lot of foreign aid to Pakistan, too. How we tried so hard to make a close friend, becoming closer to China, and now we consider India (a staunch Russian ally) our more intimate partner than Pakistan. When I asked some Pakistanis, their perception was very different; they thought the U.S. abandoned Pakistan for profit every time. Why is that perception taking ground by the day? Let's see: during 1971, when Russia was the staunch supporter of India and the U.S. was the Pakistani ally, the U.S. 7th fleet never showed up to rescue Pakistan per Nixon's pledges. When Pakistan did everything and beyond by sacrificing more than 30,000 soldiers and causing 150 billion USD in damage to their economy in assisting the American war in Afghanistan, America came up with the slogan "do more." The perception is that the U.S. turned towards India to cash in India's big population as a market share incentive. If this is true, then the U.S. policymakers should not blame Pakistan for becoming cozy with China, as Pakistan was not left with any choice but to go to China for future needs for their survival.

Missteps with Pakistan: Moreover, news and incidents like the famous quote from Musharraf that the U.S. threatened Pakistan that if Pakistan would not give support, then Pakistan would be turned into the Stone Age. The incident involved 24 Pakistani soldiers killed by the U.S.-led NATO helicopter at Salala Check post. Even recently, the former Pakistani Prime Minister Imran Khan blamed the U.S. for toppling his government. These things make me think about how hard we work to make our friends turn into foes or join our rivals, and then we complain, like naïve people, about why there is more hate towards Americans. *I will never forget the comments of a local who said America left Pakistan for India; India was a USSR and Russian ally for forty years. What type of strategic and national interest* *is that you abandon a friend for market share, or is it because of Islam? The U.S. abandoned more than 40 years of friendships for a market share; even prostitutes don't leave their regular clients like this. What good is that big population if they don't have the buying power? What good is that market share?* I mentioned to the guy that India and the U.S. are more similar in democracy, a liberal way of life, and things like culture and many liberal values, my mistake was that I asked a foolish question without thinking. *He said, well, when one has already made up their mind, then they only see what they want to see. Otherwise, what similar things? Hindus worship the cow, and millions of Americans eat Big Macs daily. Some Hindus consider human and cow pee holy, and I doubt Americans would consider pee as pure and holy. What about one God and multiple gods? As far as democracy is concerned, isn't their democracy different than your electoral college democracy, and what about human rights? Does the U.S. have human rights violations at the scale of Kashmir or what Muslims are going through? By the way, how many soldiers did India sacrifice for the U.S., like Pakistan? And if America thinks India is more like the U.S. because of Hollywood and Bollywood, does one change friends because of better expensive clothing? If so, then, there was no sincerity from the beginning.*

Addressing Misconceptions: I consider myself very logical, but I needed a proper answer to his comments, which I did not have, except that national interests supersede regional interests. However, the idea that national interests supersede regional interests is not sufficient when addressing a nation that has stood by us through thick and thin for decades. *The guy kept saying that America favored India because Israel controls American foreign policy, and since India is an Israeli friend, Israel takes care of their friends, but Americans don't. He asked, "What did Israel do for America, and what market share does Israel have for America? In fact, America gives to Israel and America even ends up getting blamed for many Israeli actions."*

I explained that he has some wrong perceptions about Israel controlling American foreign policy and some twisted market share logic. However, it made me think more about why most people believe this and why this perception is gaining strength in many parts of the world. Understanding this requires a deeper look into geopolitical dynamics and possibly exploring concepts like Space Economics to see how strategic interests are influenced and perceived globally. The concept of peace and collaboration can avoid such choices because, with collaboration, national interests and regional interests align to create a synergy effect.

Points to Ponder: When examining the relationship between the U.S. and Israel, it's essential to consider how our foreign aid policies align with our domestic priorities. Sometimes, it seems as though Israel's actions do not always reflect America's interests, leading to questions about the nature of our support. And by looking at Prime Minister Netanyahu behavior, one may get an impression, that instead of the USA giving aid to Israel, it feels like Mr. Netanyahu and Israel are the ones aiding the USA. I was particularly struck by the response during the Israel-Gaza conflict, where many Americans, especially Muslims, boycotted American companies like Starbucks, under the belief that these companies support Israel financially. While I question the validity of such claims and consider it propaganda; however, it raises an important issue: if American companies are sending profits abroad based on political or religious affiliations, should they also be investing more in addressing domestic challenges or first fix your homeland and then other places? This question isn't about targeting any American company or any other specific group. It's about a broader principle: ensuring that American businesses and policies should prioritize the needs of our own citizens. Companies have the right to allocate their resources as they see fit, but it's worth discussing whether their actions reflect a commitment to the well-being of their fellow Americans, first. Raising these questions is not about fostering division or inviting accusations.

It's about having a reasonable conversation on how best to balance our support for international allies with the pressing needs at home. By focusing on strengthening our own country, we can better support others in the long run. Let's work towards policies that reflect our shared values and ensure that our aid and support start at home, building a stronger and more unified America for all.

Influence of Lobbyists and Corporations: If lobbyists or corporations do not influence our top policymakers, is it the analysts who tell the top what the top like and want to hear?

Common Sense in Policy: Do we lose sight of common sense when we try to make things too complicated? I let the day-to-day Americans decide.

Suppose leaders start giving precedence to their political ideologies, party lines, race, religious perceptions, and generational preferences in their planning. If bosses in sensitive organizations start turning into only a promotion-oriented breed listening to lobbyists, and corporations, then national interest gradually becomes secondary.

Moral Leadership: If we teach that lying, stealing, and cheating are acceptable behaviors and applaud such comments, something is seriously wrong with our moral compass. I am referring to a talk show where former CIA Director Mike Pompeo mentioned that, and the audience clapped in response. While I understand that Pompeo may have been referring to the context of CIA agents being trained for survival, these actions should not be celebrated or discussed with pride. Such comments can influence our youth and encourage them in the wrong direction. I respect Mr. Mike Pompeo and his great service to this nation, but in my personal opinion, these types of comments should neither be made nor applauded. Instead of trying to fix other countries' moral compasses, we must first re-evaluate our own. Let's ensure that our messages and values reflect integrity and honesty. By doing so, we set a positive example for future generations and foster a society grounded in strong ethical principles.

Fixing Our Moral Compass: During the Gaza-Israel conflict, over 35,000 Palestinians, including many innocent children and women, lost their lives. The conflict began with Hamas attacking Israel, resulting in the death of 1,189 Israelis. The tragic loss of innocent lives, irrespective of their religion or nationality—be they Jews, Muslims, Christians, Hindus, Armenians, Azerbaijanis, Indians, Pakistanis, Ethiopians, Eritreans, Ukrainians, or Russians—should evoke profound sorrow in all of us. Suppose any people in any nation and we as a society feel no remorse over the death of innocents. In that case, it signals a profoundly troubling problem in our moral compass and shared human values.

Consider the recent movies *Hit Man (2023)* and *Trap (2024)*. In both films, the killers escape or manage to escape, and some of the audience responds with applause. This reaction made me question where our society is heading. The behavior of clapping and laughing at a killer's escape is alarming. When I mentioned this to a friend, expressing concern about our moral compass and how Hollywood might be influencing our youth to believe that killing is acceptable, he dismissed it, saying, "Asif, it's just a movie; it's funny; it's fun."

This mindset parallels the desensitization seen in violent video games, where killing is portrayed as entertaining. Such media can program and reshape young minds, blurring the lines between virtual actions and real-life consequences. Imagine if a policymaker were directly affected by violence inspired by these movies or games— perhaps then they would realize the urgency to address this issue. Although I hope it never happens, the probability of such incidents is increasing with each passing day as these forms of entertainment continue to influence our youth.

We must reflect on how our media consumption affects our moral compass and take proactive steps to ensure that our society values human life and empathy above all else. It's time for policymakers to recognize the potential harm and implement measures to mitigate these influences. Let's work towards a future where our media inspires positive values and fosters a compassionate and empathetic society.

Recommendations:

1. Consider regulations to check on movies and video games while respecting freedom of expression.
2. Launch public awareness campaigns to educate the public about the potential harm of media violence and video games.

3. Encourage non-violent activities by promoting participation in sports, the arts, and community service, which provide healthy outlets for energy and emotions.
4. Facilitate open discussions by creating platforms for open discussions about media violence and its potential impact on attitudes and behavior.
5. Promote positive campaigns by characters from various backgrounds in media who resolve conflicts through non-violent means.

By taking these steps, we can build a stronger and more unified America that prioritizes empathy, compassion, and the well-being of all its citizens.

Leadership Qualities: Leaders should be brave, not afraid of their shadows, and risk-takers; open to criticism and have more patience than the majority. Leaders are becoming more rating sensitive, focusing on media, what others say, international dominance, countering rivals, and fixing other countries' problems rather than the actual problems at home. Instead of looking at petty gains and limited worldly earth resources, universe resources are at our discretion. Still, some small minds cannot comprehend beyond petty gains and focus on their little corners, impossibilities, traditional geopolitical limitations, and self-fulfilling prophecies. Sometimes protocols and traditional ways don't work; fortune usually favors the brave, the risk-takers, and the first movers.

Enhancing Foreign Service Training: One of my old friends had an interesting point, which I want to add here as a suggestion. I don't know how far this is accurate or practical OR if this is still happening, but it is a great idea to establish a proper Foreign Service Academy with in-depth, regionally tailored, rigorous scenario-based training; this would involve discussing mistakes, failures, opportunities, and "what if scenarios" before the entry-level officers go to their first post—not just a few weeks of activity or a few weeks of tradecraft course. Instead, the current focus seems more on prolonged and extensive language training, which may or may not be utilized extensively during two to three years of rotations.

This comprehensive training would better prepare officers for complex situations rather than relying on short-term rotations and on-the-job training. Such preparation could lead to more effective and lasting solutions in places like Afghanistan, Iraq, and Libya. Language skills may not even be long-lasting, especially if the officer does not return to that language region or doesn't have any aptitude or intrinsic motivation for that language.

After discussing this with another friend who worked as an officer long ago, I perceived that most new officers polish their diplomatic skills through on-the-job training and shadowing experienced officers. However, these experienced officers are often extremely busy. Recruits may be much more productive if they receive extensive one to two years of well-rounded training with specific regional scenarios and discussions before going to their first post.

A superpower trying to fix complex problems in dangerous places like Afghanistan, Iraq, and Libya with yearly rotations without comprehensive training may not be very effective. Practicing and learning diplomacy through on-the-job training alone is insufficient. Officers serving one to two-year rotations in these complex places often close the chapter as soon as they leave. Why not assign highly trained and experienced officers to these places for four to five years to truly understand and solve the problems and produce results? We have some of the finest foreign service officers and some of the best soldiers; comprehensive training beforehand and this approach could maximize their potential.

Conclusion: We must critically reassess our foreign policy strategy. By focusing on our own development, leading by example, and ensuring our moral compass is intact, we can better address global challenges and foster a more positive perception of America worldwide. Let's invest in our future and collaborate with other nations to achieve common goals, rather than perpetuating conflicts that do not serve our long-term interests.

Why Do Many Muslims Perceive That Israel Controls U.S. Foreign Policy?

There is an ongoing perception, especially in some Muslim countries, that U.S. foreign policy tailors Israel's interests more than American interests. U.S. presidential hopefuls, rising policymakers, and most politicians unconditionally support Israel. Israel is our ally, and friends should support friends and partners. However, the perception is gaining strength that American leaders and policymakers tend to be more pro-Israel than pro-American.

The Question of National Loyalty: One of my friends once asked me how many generations it would take for an Armenian-American, Azerbaijani-American, Indian-American, Pakistani-American, Israeli-American, or Palestinian-American to think as an American-American and prioritize American interests. Do we even ask each other these questions?

I didn't know what to say, but it made me think: Are we Americans from different origins acting as neutral parties and American-Americans? Are we honest to ourselves and our U.S. homeland unconditionally? I am not judging anyone or implying anything, but when our presidential hopefuls give statements to support a friend or ally unconditionally, it doesn't make sense to me if we are a nation trying to uphold a high moral ground. Should we even support an ally unconditionally if our national interest, moral high ground, and goodwill are at stake? No, absolutely NOT.

Unconditional Support and Its Consequences: I would immediately take that presidential hopeful out of my books because unconditionally supporting another country puts that country above my own homeland, which is unacceptable to me. To me, it is equivalent to high treason and an un-American gesture. Supporting unconditionally gives a clear perception to other nations that our policymakers are subservient to another power at the expense of our national interest.

Changing the Perception: How can we change this perception?

Are we using common sense when some politicians give statements indicating unconditional support to any other nation, even though that nation's human rights values and ethics contradict our high moral ground? Is that leader trying to compete in their electoral college based on values, competency, and substance for that electoral area, or are they inviting influential groups to assist them because they need help? Will that help be free of cost or at the cost of our national interest?

The Cost of Foreign Aid: Should we send our taxpayers' money to assist other nations in their fights where we also become a party and eventually a collateral victim? What benefits are our taxpayers getting out of that? Could a policymaker show that as a cost-benefit analysis to some factory workers in the U.S. and convince them that this foreign aid would make the U.S. factory workers richer? Would giving foreign aid to other nations make the U.S. taxpayers' lives better in the U.S.? Will giving tremendous aid and assistance to foreign governments make our taxpayers Americans more likable around the world? Does becoming likable pay the bills and provide healthcare for our factory workers? Is it making common sense? I may be missing something.

The Need for Collaboration: Once, I was surprised to hear from a friend saying, "Some people or organizations won't collaborate even if they know they could go 1000 miles ahead with collaboration; they would instead prefer to go 100 miles ahead without collaboration as they cannot see someone different succeeding." This narrow-minded and short-term psyche shows insecurities and a defeated mindset. We must get out of that mindset to go beyond petty limitations. God made the universe and space to explore and excel beyond our imaginations. However, we still cannot move beyond the little worldly gains, waiting for old prophecies to be fulfilled for centuries. Our fears of unknowns, insecurities, and incompetence get satisfaction by focusing on impossibilities and countering rivals' perceived propaganda or future successes.

Prioritizing American Needs Over Foreign Aid

On the one hand, our policymakers keep sending foreign aid to help others, while at home, we keep piling up debt and increasing the debt ceiling. It's ironic that we have budget excuses and resource limitations for our struggling fellow Americans, yet we have the heart and pockets for foreign nations and allies. Our own citizens should be the first priority.

Embarrassing Government Shutdowns and Debt Increases: It's embarrassing that our debt-driven government has to shut down due to a lack of funds and repeatedly increase the debt ceiling. How ironic that our nation has to borrow money only to lend to other nations, neglecting our own citizens? This mismanagement reflects poorly on our priorities and fiscal responsibility.

The Rich Beggar Paradox: Our government behaves like a rich beggar, lending money to other beggars while neglecting its own family and piling up debt. This paradoxical policy needs urgent re-evaluation. Our policymakers should undergo debt counseling, and struggling Americans should hold them accountable for sending taxpayer money abroad.

Accountability and Prioritization: Whether it's Israel, Ukraine, or Egypt, those countries should fix their own problems and manage their resources effectively. We should not be responsible for their mismanagement, and our allies should not exploit our generosity. Do these allies care about struggling and homeless Americans? The priority should be clear: our policymakers must first ensure that there are no homeless people in the U.S. before considering sending foreign aid.

Taxed to the Bone: Why Hardworking Americans Are Fed Up with Foreign Aid: While working as a Chief Operating Officer and General Manager of a hotel, I frequently interacted with my staff and hardworking Americans. Time and again, I heard their frustrations when they saw news of the U.S. sending money to Ukraine and Israel. They would say, "We're working our asses off, living paycheck to paycheck. Does any other nation give us aid to improve our lives or

69

pay our bills? Why does the government tax us to give our money to others? They just keep giving our money away. Some believe that their senators and policymakers get good benefits and don't really know how the common person is struggling to balance debts and expenses."

I could see how President Trump's message resonated with these simple, hardworking Americans. I knew some of them personally; I saw their struggles with bills and debts. I understood their perspective.

Years ago, I wrote an Interest-Free Mortgage Theory and sent it to the National Science Foundation. If given the chance, I would write about how our citizens are burdened by interest rates on their small loans, shrinking their paychecks even further. Here in the land of the free, in pursuit of happiness, most of us are becoming more miserable and stressed than many people in other countries.

What have we done to ourselves? Where is the common sense? How did we end up in this mess?

Insane Common-Sense Policy: It's insane that, while we are beggars ourselves, we are making others beggars, too. What kind of common-sense policy is this? Our government needs to reprioritize and focus on the needs of American citizens first. By reallocating resources from foreign aid to domestic issues, we can address the struggles of our fellow Americans and build a stronger, more self-sufficient nation.

Are We Using Common Sense When It Comes to Abortion, Gun Violence, and Economic Disparities?

The Abortion Debate: Now that Roe vs. Wade has been overturned, taking away the right to terminate a pregnancy even if the woman is at risk of losing her life, with no exceptions for genetic abnormalities, rape, or incest. Isn't this like someone trespassing on your property, shooting at you, and you have no choice but to get shot? On one side, we are advocating for women's rights and freedom, telling the Taliban to give women their rights, but on the other side, we are trying to take that freedom away from them.

Imagine asking a staunch anti-abortion lawmaker: if God forbid, their daughter had an abnormal genetic pregnancy or was raped by a maniac, would they still stick to their anti-abortion stance? Are we missing something here? Some people may want to make it personal by invoking their religious beliefs on others, but isn't that precisely what we criticize the Taliban for doing? I'm not comparing lawmakers to the Taliban, but some media and extreme people tend to twist things, so let's use common sense.

The Gun Violence Crisis: Let's look at gun violence. Every time I see the news of a shooting, especially a school shooting, my heart goes out to the victims and their loved ones. It's devastating, and there are no words to describe the loss of life. While we tell other nations to become more tolerant and civilized, we are becoming increasingly intolerant and divided.

One of my Afghan American friends pointed out that in Afghanistan, almost every house has an AK-47, yet school shootings are practically unheard of. Why do we see such frequent shootings here in America? Is it the video games or the medications prescribed to students? Are we truly sincere in controlling gun violence? Our lawmakers are adamant about passing anti-abortion laws; I wish they would put the same effort into practical measures to prevent gun violence. Are political affiliations and money from gun manufacturers and lobbyists more important than the human values we propagate around the world? We seem so focused on solving other countries' problems that we ignore our own pressing issues.

Economic Disparities and Corporate Profiteering: The basic rules of supply and demand are important, but there is enough for everyone. Are we even trying to think outside the box? Big corporations, oil companies, pharmaceuticals, and insurance companies make enormous profits, and sometimes it seems like there is no end to profiteering. If a corporation makes billions in profit every quarter while 90% of its employees live paycheck to paycheck, something is fundamentally wrong.

Some might say I am naive and don't understand how the world works, but I leave it to ordinary people to decide. Does it make sense to them? I'm not advocating for socialism, which many media outlets might accuse me of to marginalize my points. I'm talking about companies making billions in profits thanks to their employees' hard work.

Most employees who achieve these profits are living hand-to-mouth because their wages never reflect the company's success—not even 5% to 10% bonuses are proportional to the profits. Providing fair bonuses would motivate employees and boost productivity. Yet, a traditional CEO might consider this naive. But if that's true, why do CEOs and VPs receive hefty bonuses proportional to the company's revenues?

Poor workers' salaries are never adjusted for inflation or the company's success. When we preach equality, fairness, and anti-corruption, doesn't this contradiction undermine our moral high ground? Does it make common sense?

What About Student Loans and Medical Coverage?

What About Student Loans and Medical Coverage? The United States provides billions of dollars in aid to other countries annually. In 2022 alone, the U.S. allocated nearly $74 billion in foreign aid to over 150 countries and territories; this includes substantial amounts for countries like Ukraine ($12.4 billion), Israel ($3.3 billion, and this year $26 billion in aid, with $15 billion for military assistance), and Ethiopia ($2.2 billion) (https://worldpopulationreview.com/country-rankings/us-foreign-aid-by-country) (https://usafacts.org/articles/which-countries-receive-the-most-aid-from-the-us/).

While these contributions support various geopolitical and humanitarian objectives, they raise the question of why we prioritize foreign aid over resolving domestic issues such as student loans and healthcare costs.

Prioritizing American Students: While the U.S. provides substantial foreign aid and scholarships to international students to promote American culture and build partnerships, American students are often left burdened with significant student loan debt. It is not just about the funds but about fairness and priorities.

International students benefit from programs labeled as grants or exchange initiatives, receiving financial assistance that is, in essence, supported by U.S. taxpayers. Meanwhile, the average American student graduates have over $30,000 in student loans, which can lead to decades of financial strain and hinder their economic mobility and stability.

By ensuring that American students are debt-free first, we can alleviate a major financial burden and create a more equitable system. Prioritizing our students' education and financial well-being before extending generosity abroad is not only fair but essential for fostering a strong, educated workforce that can contribute to the nation's prosperity.

The Healthcare Dilemma: The cost of insurance and medication in the U.S. is significantly higher than in many other developed countries. Unlike nations such as Canada, the U.K., and Australia, which provide universal healthcare without being labeled as socialist, the U.S. healthcare system is plagued by high costs and limited access. In 2022, healthcare spending in the U.S. reached $4.3 trillion, with individuals often facing exorbitant out-of-pocket expenses.

Lobbyists and corporations in the healthcare industry continue to resist changes that could make healthcare more affordable for all Americans. A uniform healthcare tax of 1-3% could fund a system that provides coverage for everyone, yet such proposals face stiff opposition due to the influence of these powerful groups.

A Call for Domestic Focus: If it were up to me, not a single penny would go to foreign aid once we have addressed our own critical issues. Imagine a scenario where you prioritize your neighbor's children over your own, leaving your kids to fend for themselves; this is analogous to the current situation where we fund international aid while neglecting the student debt and healthcare needs of our own citizens.

The Moral Imperative: What if those who oppose universal healthcare and debt-free education had to experience life without these necessities? It is easy to oppose reforms when one is not directly affected by the consequences. We often preach high moral values, human compassion, and ethics to the world yet fail to practice them at home. Are we following common sense, or are we merely thinking about our own interests?

In conclusion, it is crucial to re-evaluate our priorities. By focusing on resolving domestic issues such as student loans and healthcare costs, we can ensure a better future for all Americans before extending our generosity abroad.

Exploring Double Standards: Same-Sex Marriage vs. Polygamy

Why is Same-Sex Marriage OK, but Polygamy and Polyandry Are Unacceptable?

Freedom of speech and religion are fundamental tenets of our Constitution. The Declaration of Independence emphasizes liberty, freedom, and the pursuit of happiness. If our policymakers, human rights activists, and liberals strongly advocate for same-sex marriages, why do they oppose consenting adults practicing polygamy or polyandry?

Private Matters and Public Hypocrisy: One of my liberal Democrat friends was teasing our Republican friend, asking how conservative Trump supporters who consider themselves bearers of high moral values could still vote for President Trump even after his comments about proudly "grabbing pussies." How do 30 million Republicans vote for Trump? Our Republican friend reacted by mentioning President Clinton's affair with Monica Lewinsky. I asked both of them only two questions.

Why do we want to focus on others' private matters, matters between consenting adults, even if they are public figures? We should have no business in the private lives of our citizens' personal matters and sexual preferences. We should focus on issues like the economy, employment, building infrastructure, law and order, healthcare, education, defense, and industry. Secondly, what kind of logic is it that consenting men and women should be allowed same-sex marriage, but polygamy or polyandry for consenting men and women is considered taboo and illegal? I am surprised that some Western activists are vocal and adamant about supporting same-sex marriages in some Muslim countries in the name of human rights and human liberties, but the same human rights activists are reluctant to discuss polygamy between consenting men and women practiced in Muslim countries being brought to Western countries.

Contradictory Attitudes: Why are the same patriotic and brave liberal voters not okay with polygamy within the sacred bounds of some religions but okay with same-sex marriages? Why is flirting and infidelity not considered as big of a taboo as same-sex marriages or polygamy and polyandry? Why are there limits to freedom of religion where the matter is between consenting men and women and a private matter not hurting anyone considered taboo? Why can some American Mormons and Muslims not exercise their freedom of religion rights? Why do we just fit the freedom of religion clause to media preferences or lobbyists' desires? Or is there some marketing and profitability angle that average consumers cannot foresee?

If both consenting men and women are okay with it and hurting no one, and if polygamy is economically, socially, and in some instances medically and motivationally beneficial to some, then why the fuss?

The Case for Polygamy: If consenting adults agree to polygamy and it brings economic, social, and sometimes medical benefits, why is there opposition? If same-sex marriages are allowed, why shouldn't polygamy or polyandry be permitted among consenting people? Polygamy is legal in some Muslim countries like Qatar, the UAE, Saudi Arabia, Bahrain, and Pakistan. If China's human rights violations against Uyghurs warrant condemnation, shouldn't these countries also be condemned if polygamy is so objectionable?

In a Muslim country, I asked a man with two wives how his first wife permitted it. His response was insightful: *"If my wife hadn't allowed it, I wouldn't have. I didn't marry for sex only, which others always think; I had such circumstances where my second wife became immense support and helped my first wife and her kids. It helped our family, and both wives made the family economically and socially much stable, and it positively affected our lives. I don't care what the world thinks; it was beneficial to my wives and me. The West would never understand it. The West perceives polygamy as very bad and Muslims as unfavorable; even Mormons are looked at differently by most. The media only promotes same-sex marriages because high-ups and money guys favor that, but nobody considers how polygamy would reduce cheating, infidelity, and other ills. Practically it is load-sharing, cost-sharing, responsibilities sharing code of life between sensible adults. It made our family more stable economically and socially."* Although I disagreed with some of his points, he made valid arguments.

Reflecting on Values: Perhaps same-sex marriages provide emotional support to same-sex couples, and polygamy could offer the same to those in such relationships. Maybe polygamy and polyandry could reduce divorce rates. The media often twists comments to highlight negativities. If we play the finger-pointing game, we can find many negatives about single lifestyles or unhappy marriages.

We celebrate Pride Week and Month, raise flags for gays and lesbians, and promote same-sex marriages. Why don't we also support married couples, single moms, and single dads trying their best? Where is the common sense? Do we have less sympathy for struggling single parents than for gays and lesbians? Do we only promote values favored by mainstream media and corporations?

Hypocrisy in Corporate Policies: Some organizations insist their employees wear pride shirts and publicly shame those who refuse. Why not put the same effort into promoting "keep the marriage" shirts or "support single mom" shirts? Stop this hypocrisy, please.

Conclusion: The debate on same-sex marriage versus polygamy highlights inconsistencies in our advocacy for freedom and human rights. By re-evaluating our stance on these issues, we can strive for a more inclusive and fair society.

Are We Okay with the New Norm?

Only a true friend speaks up when something is wrong and offers constructive suggestions. If I could offer advice to President Trump, I would suggest not distancing minorities. People appreciate your boldness, straightforwardness, and blunt approach, but it's important to remember that overly candid remarks can damage your public image, even in private conversations. Good American values and ethics still apply, even in the locker room. Our wives, daughters, sisters, and mothers don't become faceless there. It's not about criticism for the sake of it but about engaging in a constructive dialogue that can lead to positive change.

Are we becoming hypocrites by saying whatever we want in private but hiding behind an artificial mask of societal values in public? If we accept this as the norm, we shouldn't be surprised when our kids grow up thinking it's okay to behave inappropriately, like mistreating interns or making disrespectful comments about women.

Refugees, foreigners, immigrants, Muslims, Mexicans, etc., are not to blame for changing our values or culture; we are responsible for these new norms ourselves. If we want to uphold our cherished values, we must consistently reflect them publicly and privately.

Is Downsizing a Deceptive Indicator of Leadership Incompetence?

The Problem with Outsourcing Solutions: Do we jump on the bandwagon because of the glitter and hype some consultants create? These consultants try to fix company problems in a few hours or weeks, believing they know more than those who work there day and night. First of all, the leadership of such an organization should be ashamed of bringing in an outsider to fix a problem they couldn't fix themselves. It reflects a lack of vision and competence when leaders don't know how to fix their own house and have to ask a neighbor, who has never been there before, to come and find the problem.

Questioning the Profitability of Downsizing: Are the profitability numbers for shareholders, derived from cost-saving through downsizing and job cuts, a realistic measure of success? We have elevated many CEOs who saved money through job cuts and by outsourcing manufacturing to countries like China, India, and other developing nations. This suggests that the leader was shortsighted and incompetent; such measures only show artificial gains on the balance sheets. Cutting hundreds to thousands of jobs at the lower level instead of replacing a few at the top would save much more money. If the CEO and top management cannot utilize the workforce to diversify or find new market niches, it is the leadership's fault, not the workers. What our corporate pundits do is cut jobs and reward the incompetent top executives. They believe that taking the livelihood of 1,000 families instead of firing the top incompetent leader is called productivity and saving money. Instead of firing the incompetent commander of an inefficient army, they fire the poor soldiers who follow the commander's orders. If the general couldn't train or effectively maneuver his forces, he should be the one fired, not the troops.

The Jack Welch Approach: A Flawed Strategy? Someone told me that Jack Welch fires the lowest-performing 10% of any team annually. But what about CEOs? Is it not the CEO's fault if they couldn't make that 10% lowest-performing group productive again? Are we deceiving the shareholders legally by inflating the numbers through cutting the jobs of hardworking people because management didn't know how to utilize those HR resources effectively? Common sense would say it's the lack of foresight of the top management, not knowing how to make the organization productive and how to use that 10% workforce that they laid off. We are saving money by covering our incompetency. Many CEOs would follow the same path as a media-awarded CEO without thinking outside the box.

The Real Cost of Leadership Failure: In conclusion, downsizing as a profitability tactic is often a deceptive indicator of leadership incompetence. It's not the workers who fail; it's the leaders who fail to utilize their resources effectively. Cutting jobs may temporarily boost the bottom line, but it ultimately reflects a deeper issue: a lack of vision and competence at the top. To truly succeed, leaders need to think beyond short-term gains and focus on sustainable, innovative solutions that benefit everyone involved.

Should a Free Market Regulated Economy Worry About Inflation?

Increased prices for fuel, consumer goods, and daily commodities are surging, leading to fears of inflation and causing the Federal Reserve to adjust interest rates but raising those interest rates are affecting business.

The Free-Market Economy Debate: Are we really a free market economy? Technically, in a free market economy, prices adjust according to supply and demand, and we should not try to control either. Did our economic moves hasten or avoid the debacles of Freddie Mac and Fannie Mae?

Questioning Traditional Economic Measures: Are we using the same old formula of expanding or contracting the economy by controlling a simple interest rate? During and after COVID, a COVID sensitivity analysis leading to a COVID sensitivity factor or constant should have been integrated into the interest rate equation. This would account for ongoing manufacturing operations and correct the artificial supply-demand paradox, explaining pre- and post-COVID demand and supply curves for error corrections. Usually, interest rates are increased to cool down the economy and businesses to control inflation. However, do we need to slow down businesses that were already adversely affected during and after COVID? Many businesses closed during and after COVID, and they couldn't find enough people to work. How would an increased interest rate help those struggling businesses return to their lifeline? How would an increased interest rate help a closed business start up again by borrowing money at a much higher cost, which would then be passed on to consumers? And nobody even talks about those stimulus checks that made matters worse, helped creating an artificial inflation, which did not follow the traditional inflation rules and patterns, and made FEDs fluctuating interest-rate-control-weapon ineffective, instead turned it into a propaganda among two major parties in the U.S. government.

Impact on Mortgages and Average Consumers: How would higher interest rates impact mortgage payments? How would higher mortgage rates help the majority of poor and average people who already struggle to afford mortgage rates, rents, or cope with rising prices?

Higher interest rates increase the cost of borrowing, leading to higher mortgage payments. This can significantly affect poor and average-income individuals who already struggle with housing affordability, whether through mortgage rates or rents, amidst rising prices.

The inflation we're experiencing partly stems from COVID-19 disruptions, which severed supply chains, created order backlogs, and affected labor availability and training. Simply controlling interest rates to curb inflation overlooks these complexities. The unique post-COVID environment has created what I term "FAD inflation"—a temporary spike resembling a fashion trend. Traditional measures like raising interest rates may not address these root causes and could even backfire, mistaking FAD inflation for traditional inflation.

Cooling the economy through higher interest rates might harm small businesses already under stress. Stock prices remain below pre-COVID levels, and many average investors are cautious. Insisting on cooling the economy in such a scenario seems counterintuitive. We should instead harness the power of the free-market economy that we advocate globally, allowing market forces to drive recovery and growth.

Why are we so adamant about cooling down the economy when many average investors are already playing conservatively? Why don't we believe in the power of the free-market economy that we preach to the world? Where is the common-sense?

Thinking Outside the Box: Sometimes standard protocols don't work, and we have to think outside the box and consider environmental factors that weren't part of the equation affecting the traditional formula before. Let me re-emphasize that we are trying to cool down an economy that is already going through turbulence, and we are trying to cool down businesses that are already down.

Evaluating Current Measures: Are we doing the right thing by raising interest rates to cool down the economy for average consumers, who are already in a cash crunch?

Alternative Measures: In this post-COVID dilemma, instead of increasing interest rates, can't we focus on measures that would help average consumers?

For instance, implementing a four-day work week to save fuel and utility costs, restricting imports (especially luxury items), and limiting profit margins on products and services. Instead of thinking conventionally, think unconventionally by encouraging local manufacturing with cheap or interest-free loans to drive prices down.

Addressing the Car Shortage: During and immediately after COVD, there was already a car shortage. From my understanding, President Biden emphasized people buying electric cars, but how could they afford a $60K electric car when they couldn't afford even a cheaper non-electric one? Furthermore, high inflation rates mean that people were worse off unless income increases at the same rate. Salaries don't increase proportionately to inflation, but big businesses increase their profit margins proportionately. So, it's only possible if the $60K electric car loans are interest-free for the first three to five years with other incentives that make it affordable for average buyers, aligning with President Biden's eco-friendly ambitions. These initiatives would keep struggling businesses running and even generate new employment. On the other hand, even with inflation, saving fuel and energy costs like mentioned above, these strategies would have decreased the inflation havoc for the average consumer. Common sense suggests strategies like these may work more effectively in these extraordinary circumstances than just playing with interest rates.

Conclusion: Something along the lines of developmental economics, such as Space Economics initiatives mentioned in this book moving toward the next generation of the industrial revolution, may have the answers.

TRILLION DOLLAR PROJECT: REVITALIZING THE ECONOMY THROUGH SPACE ECONOMICS

Background: What is space economics, and how can it revive the post-COVID-19 economy?

A few years ago, while working at the US Embassy in Azerbaijan, I coordinated the first NASA Space Apps Hackathon in Azerbaijan at the ADA University. This event highlighted the remarkable power of global collaboration. Teams from various countries and disciplines united to tackle Earth and space challenges, demonstrating the immense potential of collective intelligence. This experience inspired me to consider whether a project could unite the world, eliminate unemployment, and foster global harmony over limited resources, all while boosting corporate profits and public well-being.

With my background in Economics, Project Management, and Complexity, I started writing in my free time about a space project as a hobby and as fiction at first. Later, I realized it is very much doable and a concept that can change the world. I called the concept space economics, where I envisioned a world where space mining, satellite-based technologies, and space tourism could drive technological advancements and create new industries.

Concept and Vision: Space economics involves leveraging space-related activities to stimulate economic growth on Earth. This includes initiatives like space mining, satellite-based technologies, and developing new markets in space tourism and manufacturing. These ventures could create jobs, spur technological advancements, and drive new industries, providing a substantial boost to the global economy.

Here's how space economics can help revitalize the post-COVID-19 economy:

1. **Job Creation:** The space industry can generate millions of jobs, ranging from high-tech engineering and manufacturing positions to roles in research, development, and support services.
2. **Technological Innovation:** Investment in space technologies drives advancements in related fields, such as telecommunications, materials science, and renewable energy, leading to broader economic benefits.
3. **Global Collaboration:** Space projects often require international cooperation, fostering peaceful relations and shared goals among nations, and promoting global stability.
4. **Resource Utilization:** Space exploration opens up access to vast resources, such as minerals from asteroids and solar energy from space-based systems, reducing competition for Earth's limited resources.
5. **Economic Diversification:** By developing a robust space economy, we diversify our economic activities beyond traditional industries, making the global economy more resilient to shocks and disruptions.

The TRILLION DOLLAR PROJECT aims to harness the potential of space economics to stimulate economic recovery and growth. By uniting governments, corporations, and academic institutions in a collaborative effort, we can create a sustainable and prosperous future that benefits all of humanity.

The Journey: I shared my ideas with esteemed professors, including one of my mentors, Dr. Mirsad Hadzikadic, a Professor of Complexity who ran for a seat in the Presidency of Bosnia and Herzegovina and currently leads the Platform for Progress party. He encouraged me to showcase this concept in an agent-based simulation for the Complexity Journal, but circumstances did not allow for it.

Despite sharing the article with renowned magazines and institutions, it was often deemed too futuristic or out of scope. I even tried sending the article to famous entrepreneurs like Elon Musk and Richard Branson, hoping to capture their interest. Some friends laughed at my efforts, warning that famous individuals don't read unsolicited articles and that my ideas might be copied without acknowledgment. However, my intention was never about money or fame but about making a meaningful impact.

If someone like Elon Musk or a bold policymaker happens to read it and it clicks, then the world will be a much better place. I truly believe that a bold and visionary leader, someone like Elon Musk or President Trump, has the guts to initiate this kind of mega collaborative project with both friends and foes.

Eventually, one of my father's friends and my father himself listened to my concept. Once they understood, they advised me to write a book to benefit the common man—the regular Joe. So, I wrote the article at the end of the book for policymakers and top leaders, hoping that someday, someone might read it. I published it at my own expense, without my name, to avoid bias and seek genuine consideration of the idea.

The feedback from academics, colleagues, and a few policymakers was overwhelmingly positive, recognizing the significant potential of space economics. They encouraged me to keep trying, despite the challenges of finding bold leaders and visionary entrepreneurs like Elon Musk to bring this idea to fruition.

The Need for Visionary Leadership: Transforming this concept into reality requires visionary leadership willing to take high risks. Traditional policymakers often lack the foresight or willingness to embrace groundbreaking ideas, constrained by conventional thinking and bureaucratic inertia. Engaging dynamic leaders in the private sector and fostering public-private partnerships is crucial.

Missed Opportunities and Future Potential: Had a mega collaborative space project been initiated earlier, it might have mitigated geopolitical tensions, such as the Russian-Ukraine conflict, by shifting focus towards a unifying global endeavor. The reluctance of traditional policymakers to accept and act on visionary ideas highlights a significant gap in strategic planning.

Moving Forward: The potential of space economics is vast and untapped. While this article serves as a conceptual framework, the operational details require collaborative input from experts across various fields. The goal is to refine and transform these ideas into actionable strategies that can be implemented globally.

Summary Before the Article Itself: I wrote this article on space economics as an alternative solution for America and other global powers to embark on a mega project leveraging peace and collaboration instead of conflict. By combining resources, this revolutionary approach can revitalize the post-COVID-19 economy. However, it requires bold leadership and a willingness to embrace high-risk, high-reward initiatives. The journey from concept to reality is complex, but with the right visionaries at the helm, it holds the promise of a transformative impact on our world.

Before I start my article, I want to explain Keynesian Economics and the multiplier effect in a story that everyone can understand. The reason I am doing this is because many who read my article or the book suggested explaining Keynesian Economics and the multiplier effect for those who don't know anything about them, as my article refers to them a lot.

Understanding Keynesian Economics: A Story for Everyone

Imagine a small town called "**Imagineville.**" Imagineville was a bustling place where people were happy and businesses thrived. But one day, a terrible storm hit the town. The storm caused a lot of damage, and suddenly, Imagineville wasn't so prosperous anymore. Businesses closed, people lost their jobs, and the town fell into a deep recession.

Now, there are two groups of economists who have different ideas about how to help the town recover. The first group is called the Classical Economists. They believe that the economy is like a rubber band. Even if it gets stretched or squeezed, it will eventually go back to its original shape on its own. So, they say, "Don't worry! Just wait, and Imagineville will bounce back by itself!" (...such as from depression or recession to recovery to growth to expansion etc.)

But there's another group of economists who have a different idea. This group is led by a smart and thoughtful man named Lord Keynes. Lord Keynes says, "Why should we wait for Imagineville to recover on its own when we can help it get back on its feet faster?" He believes in some catalyst which he called a "stimulus" to kick-start the economy.

Lord Keynes suggests that the government should step in and start building things like hospitals, roads, and schools. He explains that when the government hires workers to build these projects, those workers will get paid wages. Imagine this: there's a group of workers building a new road in Imagineville. Every week, they get paid for their hard work.

Now, what do these workers do with their wages? They go to the local grocery store to buy food for their families. The grocery store owner is happy because more people are buying food, so he hires more staff and orders more supplies. The grocery store workers then take their paychecks and maybe buy new clothes for their kids. The clothing store owner, in turn, sees more customers and hires more workers. And so on and so on.

This chain reaction of spending is what Lord Keynes calls the "multiplier effect." It's like a snowball rolling down a hill, getting bigger and bigger. One small action – like building a road – can create a big impact on the whole town. Money starts to flow through Imagineville again, businesses reopen, and more jobs are created.

Thanks to Lord Keynes' idea, Imagineville comes out of its recession much faster than if everyone had just waited for things to get better on their own. The town's economy starts to grow and expand, bringing back the happiness and prosperity that everyone loved.

So, the next time you hear about Keynesian Economics, remember the story of Imagineville. It's all about giving the economy a little push when it's down, to help it stand up and start running again. And that's how you can turn a tough situation into a success story!

Article Abstract

Space Economics is an emerging concept that can play a crucial role in global peace and partnership among world powers. Space Economics can be more lucrative than FDI (Foreign Direct Investment), traditional stimulus packages, and conventional Economies of Scale combined. Is there a way where, instead of tightening national boundaries and imposing tariffs on foreign competitors to support local businesses, local businesses become part of a global collaborative project? Can Keynesian economics principles help nations team up instead of negatively competing and not worrying about limited resources or the supply and demand problems? The space domain can initiate the era of collaboration that could take the US, UK, and the EU and competitors like Russia, China, and others away from confrontation and towards something more potent than even the Chinese one-belt-one-road initiative. On the contrary, the Chinese one-belt-one-road initiative can become part of this project. COVID-19 affected world economies substantially and contributed to rising unemployment. Is there a better solution to address global unemployment issues? Space Economics doesn't mean building only spaceships or space colonies on the Moon or Mars. The Keynesian multiplier in emerging space economics from a joint space project can turn around the post-COVID-19 economy, avoid possible economic depression, contentious economics, and the next cold war.

Keywords: Keynesian Economics, Space Economics, Economic Revival, Multiplier Effect, Post COVID-19 Economy.

INTRODUCTION

The COVID-19 fiasco shattered world economies to an unprecedented level. The world may not realize the aftermath of COVID-19 and some of the ripple effects for many years to come. Is there any quick fix to recover world economies? Many analysts think economic conditions may force some political pundits to think of wars as an alternative to divert economic and political attention from their respective home fronts. Some think of injecting stimulus packages as a defibrillator to jump-start the struggling economy, neglecting that Keynesian Economics may not do the magic on failing projects that follow traditional supply and demand curves, especially with high government deficits. "However, after four stimulus plans from 2008 to 2010 failed to create net new jobs, a revulsion to more spending emerged." (Rickards, 2011).

Globalization and Its Challenges: When things did not turn around per globalization visionaries, Dani Rodrik mentioned in his book, "The Globalization Paradox," that globalization backfired. Some suggested instilling nationalism and restricting globalization to ensure the proper allocation of limited resources within their national boundaries, neglecting the power of collaboration and reinvention as a better way to progress. For those who couldn't benefit from globalization, globalization led to confrontation and fear, prompting a return to isolationist strategies. Collaboration doesn't mean one nation taking undue advantage of another nation. Governments can collaborate and eliminate boundaries, and at the same time, countries can keep their nationalistic ideologies, borders, and sovereignty intact. Some are predicting new chaos with an inevitable new cold war. Some staunchly believe in their respective religious interpretations through self-righteous men and propagate the stereotyping of end-day scenarios leading to more hopelessness instead of proactivity, collaboration, and exploration.

Economic Competition and Rising Tensions: Economic competition and rising frictions to gain dominance in new technological advancements have started showing visible tensions between economic giants like the U.S. and China, and rising tensions in the Caucasus and Russian boundary lines. Neglecting the fact that there are two different systems and ideologies, one may be more focused on personal liberties and a free-market economy; the other focuses more on control and order. Every nation wants to safeguard its interests. Both sides are perceiving and portraying the other side as damaging and counterproductive. Both are trying to show themselves better than the other by elaborating their rival's perceived ills, and even some policymakers and media are determined to add fuel to the fire. Can something create the middle ground or acceptable turf for this kind of scenario? How can we turn the possibility of this kind of contentious economics into collaborative economics to avoid another cold war? Is there a solution to this perceived animosity? Is there a solution to unemployment, economic fears, and this globalization paradox?

The Keynesian Solution: The solution to unemployment, economic fears, and the globalization dilemma may lie in one of the dimensions of Keynesian Economics by tapping into unlimited hidden resources without shortage. For national interest, a nation may activate that Keynesian cascade effect through something parallel to mythical BLACK OPS deep funds (Broad, 2008). Why not allocate deep funds to jump-start a massive space program to avoid not only a possible U.S. recession but also a global economic depression? This initiative could be more powerful than the Chinese One Belt One Road initiative (Ferdinand, 2016). On the contrary, U.S. collaboration with the Chinese One Belt One Road initiative could perfectly align to jump-start such a project, resulting in the U.S. benefiting more than even China. Instead of countering Chinese One Belt One Road or CPEC projects, working together would yield far greater benefits than the energy and resources expended to counter the rival.

Mega Space Projects: Can some kind of black-ops fund for a mega space project (in a contained way) save collapsing economies without inflation and deflation repercussions? Profit-seeking and economic control do not mean that collaboration among world economic powers for a stable, peaceful, and economically progressive world is not possible. A mega space project by the U.S. can unleash the power of Keynesian Economic principles in creating future jobs, transforming current technological advancements to the next level of a knowledge-based economy, and further developing untapped human capital, thus initiating the next industrial revolution. Allies willingly becoming part of this venture can lead to a new techno-economic boom beyond current economic perceptions of wealth. As a byproduct, developing countries joining this kind of project would automatically build their economies in the realms of developmental economics.

Challenges to Space Economics: However, some orthodox politicians, especially conventional decision-makers of controlled economies and typical intelligence personnel worldwide, may be the first ones to oppose this kind of project because Space Economics demands resources used for collaboration, transparency, and proactive alliances to benefit all parties, which is contrary to the traditional medieval way of gaining an edge over rivals through covert operations, negativity, and finding shortcuts. Some corporations, lobbyists, and think tanks may also be reluctant to propagate this idea because they might perceive this kind of development, collaboration, and peace as contrary to their core beliefs and current business models.

The Future of Space Economics: Nobody is asking to reveal their business tricks and secret ingredients; the focus is not on giving a free ride to others. Space Economics focuses on unlimited space resources, which indicates a different supply and demand curve than traditional demand and supply curves due to the endless and vast resources space provides. One needs to develop new technologies, a different mindset, and creative methodologies to harness those resources. Whichever nation harnesses the space resources would have the quantum leap, not the countries focused on limited worldly technologies. Space Economics can be a new type of developmental economics even for highly developed nations to speed up the technological revolution to the next level to create needed jobs and innovation that curbs frustration and division and gives hope and opportunity to become part of something bigger than all of us.

Unemployment creates hopelessness, reduces quality of life, and leads to extremism and even terrorism.

Collaboration Over Competition: Instead of the traditional thinking of disrupting rivals' progress as an ingredient of success, maligning each other, or trying to get ahead by copying or sabotaging others, it is time to think out of the box to assist each other in something bigger than all of us. A mega project like this will divert petty fights, cheap politics, religious end-day scenarios, a conspiracy mindset, and efforts to foment insurgencies and 5th/6th Generation warfare on rivals. The U.S. and Russia competed in the space race, which triggered progress in many domains; imagine if that space race had been a collaborative project from the beginning, how fast and how far the world could have gone. Fears, negatives, and jealousy of incompetent rivals would always be there. Currently, the U.S. is the only superpower, and others may always envy the success or status of the best. Instead of wasting resources on countering the jealous and their insecurities, the BEST should focus on continuing to build and collaborating with those who want to collaborate; the test of time will prove the impact of the steady progress.

Progress and Security: Security and caution are best practices, but the steady progress with lightning speed focusing on one's development would widen the gap of competence. Instead of entangling with the rivals' petty and negative moves and keep adding additional security layers, one should focus on increasing competence and the speed of progress. Once the competent party's train of progress catches momentous speed, adversaries won't be able to catch up to that progress. The BEST can offer the world to join them in this Space Venture and progress with the BEST, or the rivals can miss this train of opportunity.

Learning from History: So many Empires came and disappeared and so many wars. Wise ones should learn from past mistakes. However, humankind makes the same mistakes again. The same traditional mentality, mistrust, suspicion, and perception of negativity is the conventional norm because it is easy to look toward negatives and blame others. Space Economics is a challenging and demanding thing to propagate, and it is also hard to imagine rivals working together by putting aside the generational memories of bias, suspicion, and hate. Only a bold and wise leader with vision would give collaboration a chance for an actual win-win situation.

Conclusion: Can a creative economic strategy of collaboration overcome all limitations, issues, and objections? The space domain can fit all that. With Space Economics, nations can progress through globalization while keeping their governments, identities, and national boundaries sovereign for the greater good. Collaboration doesn't mean changing one's culture, identity, values, and norms. Collaboration means having a partnership to combine resources, workforce, and efforts to speed up progress to a level that would have taken much longer otherwise. Space exploration and space mining are some of the domains where Keynesian Economics would work even if there is a considerable government deficit. Can complexity and economic experts unravel space economics' potential benefits from its inception phase to the operational level?

Statement of the Problem

Rising unemployment rates and high inflation are persistent problems for world economies. In some places, high unemployment rates provoke short-cut solutions of isolation blended with extreme nationalism and tariffs, leading to new cold-war fronts among regional players, and sometimes a hidden or confrontational tussle between the U.S., Russia, and rising powers like China. Traditional thinking may suggest the start of another cold war, dividing the world into two or three blocks, where each block tries to hamper the other's progress through facts or propaganda. Alternatively, peace and collaboration among all blocks could lead to a synergy effect, curbing unemployment issues and economic fears for good.

Is Space Economics the Answer?

What is Space Economics, and how can Space Economics revive the post-COVID-19 shattered world economies?

MOTIVATION AND PURPOSE OF THIS ARTICLE

Motivation and Purpose of This Article: This article explores alternative economic solutions that can generate unrivaled employment and transform a potential economic depression into a thriving economy through Keynesian Economics, despite the ongoing COVID-19 debacle. Moreover, a mega collaborative space project among rival powers like the U.S., China, and the EU (may exclude Russia till Russian-Ukraine war is over) can help avoid a cold war. The synergy of peace and cooperative economics can generate more benefits for all than contentious economics or wars. One can imagine the thrill, adventure, and exploration this project may lead to; moreover, how many new fields of study and innovations would be prompted by this venture. How many new processes and technologies would be revolutionized on Earth, providing benefits not even imagined before?

Framework

The History of Economic Exploration: Space Economics is an emerging field dealing with space research, space exploration, and developing products on Earth for space. Throughout history, various empires expanded their territories by exploring uncharted waters for economic gain. Whether it was the Romans, Vikings, Muslims, British, Dutch, French, Russians, or modern-day Americans, the aim was always to secure available and limited resources for their populace's benefit and maintain supremacy over their rivals. Constantly changing environments and unforeseen events affect supply and demand predictions unexpectedly; world resources are not unlimited.

Ethics and Economics in the Modern World: Every nation propagates slogans of humanity and ethics, but nowadays, market share and profitability ratios, under the guise of national security, often take precedence over universally accepted ethical and humanitarian standards. However, the space domain can change all that traditional thinking and fears of limitation by initiating economic progression based on the principles of Keynesian Economics.

The Potential of Space Economics: Considering the vastness of space, boundless dominion, and unlimited space resources, nations can quickly start a technological transformation to the next level, which currently, one can only see in science fiction movies. Only bold and visionary leaders may comprehend the cascade effect and benefits of this type of endeavor. The space domain can change the supply and demand rules that average businesses and traditional economies follow.

Applications of Space Economics: Whether it is building satellites for imagery or data analysis, creating next-level jet propulsion, evaluating landscapes for creative agriculture, prolific urban planning, precision mining in far-flung corners of the Earth, or the next level marketing or dumping unrecyclable waste on desolate, uninhabitable planets, space economics is the beginning of a new kind of economics that would benefit any nation.

The Future of Space Projects: Space travel, space/moon/ asteroid mining, space tourism, space trade, and space colonization are not even in the picture yet. One of my friends working for a space company mentioned that China is already aggressively working on moon and asteroid mining. So, if U.S. policymakers, leaders, and entrepreneurs do not put their act together and collaborate to take the lead, nations like China will. And China will have allies like Iran, Turkey, Russia, and old American friends like Pakistan in their adventures. So, do we want another cold war? Do we want to work together and take the lead, or do we want to divide the world here on Earth and in space too? When will we learn from our mistakes?

When will we overcome our ego, selfish thinking, impossibility thinking, and negativities and start working on possibilities?

Call to Action: Who would dare to take the risk to go beyond conventional thinking, initiate this kind of unprecedented collaboration, and make a quantum leap by becoming the first mover? In this kind of venture, the first mover can reap the most rewards and respect, and the world would follow their lead. Nations like the U.S. or the UK can retake the lead and prove once again their leadership mantle.

Ongoing Projects

"Amazon recently announced Project Kuiper. It would put more than 3,000 satellites into orbit to provide high-speed Internet to up to 4 billion new customers.

Meanwhile, SpaceX is launching Starlink to put nearly 12,000 satellites into low-earth orbit. Facebook is reportedly working on satellites, too. And that's just for surfing the web anywhere on earth. Amazon CEO Jeff Bezos says he's personally spending more than $1 billion each year to fund his other enterprise. Blue Origin is building rockets and landing modules to take people to the moon. Elon Musk has Mars in his sights with SpaceX. And then there's space tourism and asteroid mining. Some founders even dream of the day when ventures on other planets will disrupt lowly Earth businesses." (O'Sullivan, 2019).

Why is it a Necessity?

The space domain can become a profitable area that can unite the world without rivalries, leading to development, production, and expansion without the fear of diminishing demand or consumption issues. Resources needed for space would optimize exploration and innovation on Earth first, and the byproducts and services through collaboration would generate enormous prosperity and employment. One can integrate all the skilled and unskilled workforce into developing the boundless space dominion.

Global Collaboration and Job Creation: World leaders may not worry about not having enough jobs or not creating jobs for everyone. Collaboration among nations for space projects would considerably reduce cutthroat competition among rival nations, fights for quotas, and even labor shortages. Problems like illegal and undocumented workers may become issues of the past. Emerging concepts like recycling and dumping waste on desolate planets, asteroid mining, and building infrastructures on planets like Mars would give birth to new technologies, warehousing, logistics, and transportation concepts.

Diplomacy and Peace Initiatives: Peace offerings and the opening of diplomatic channels between Israel and the UAE, Bahrain, and other nations mark the beginning of a new era. COVID-19 has reminded the world that no part can be immune to the other, no matter how far apart. A mega collaborative space economics project, blessed by world powers like the US, UK, China, Russia, and the EU, can bring arch-rivals like Pakistan and India, Saudi Arabia and Iran, Israel and Palestine, and Armenia and Azerbaijan to the same table, working together for an economic vision and prosperity never imagined before. The demand and supply curves of space economics have the potential to accommodate everyone.

But who will initiate this chain reaction? The sooner someone starts, the better the world will become, realizing what it has been missing. Otherwise, to capture resources and prove supremacy, incidents like the Ukraine-Russia conflict and Israel attacked by Hamas and Gaza destroyed by Israel, resulting in thousands of innocent civilians and children's deaths, will keep happening.

Transforming Militaries into Peacekeepers: Instead of rival militaries like the US vs. Russia/China, India vs. Pakistan, or Israelis vs. Iran taunting each other, world armies can be transformed into forces for maintaining order, providing protection services, training, logistical support, and security for collaborative space ventures. Armed forces are always perceived as better in taking risks, providing superior support services, and excelling in research and development capabilities. Indeed, there would be no match for a unified military force in establishing bases to initiate the colonization of any inhabitable planets with discipline and uniform standards across the board. And only a unified world military would be the optimal answer to a future mega catastrophic event, such as an asteroid hitting Earth or neutralizing a rogue AI against humanity. By uniting resources and putting aside differences, ego, and greed, space dominion can tackle the unemployment problem and may even eliminate wars from Earth for a very long time to come. The vastness of the space domain can create unlimited supply and demand; space economics would not follow the traditional supply and demand curves.

"Looking to the stars and beyond, we can find all of the commodities, land, and resources we need to fuel economic growth. Space provides an apparently infinite supply of materials and energy that enterprises can use to build and expand, with less carbon emissions and environmental concerns than are involved in terrestrial capitalism." (Ryan, 2020). Revenues from the space would fund the research and development activities on earth to counter future pandemics and natural calamities. *"Such activities could help solve Earth's most pressing problems and foster a space industry that sustains itself financially." (Bennett, 2019).* A unified space dominion to access unlimited resources is possible through a joint global space venture—a real win-win scenario where world militaries, governments, and economies join forces while also maintaining their unique identities and sovereignty.

What Can It Achieve?

1. This type of collaborative economic system can supersede current capitalism, communism, religious and national extremism, and counter some of the isolation, fear, and hate phobias.
2. The dormant domain of space has the potential to integrate the Keynesian model, where rival states will not compete with each other but work towards a common theme of exploration

for economic synergy, providing financial stability to all nations collaborating in this venture.

3. This type of collaborative space economics would develop knowledge economies and a skilled workforce, leading to employment bliss in emerging fields through research areas never explored before.

4. This venture generates employment stability by providing products, byproducts, and services in an unending profitable domain without fear of rivals for a long time to come (unless the partners in the venture are not sincere or transparent with each other).

5. Nations would not fight with each other like vultures to secure FDI ventures or sell their products for revenue streams to support their economic lifelines. Countries would also not make cheap products for repeated sales to keep their factories running.

6. In the last 30 years, America spent more than 14.2 trillion dollars on wars. In 2008, Wall Street and Corporate America lost trillions of dollars. A fraction of that money could have developed the space industry.

7. Space is the frontier that would set aside all differences for a common goal, without competing for petty, timely gains, but looking for something greater beyond our imagination—a true synergy effect.

8. Working on a shared mission addressing common fears and mutual benefits in exploring the unknown to establish human outreach to the next level is motivation enough to reduce religious, cultural, and ethnic frictions to a minimal level. This is something that most leaders might not comprehend now, and which prophets had a hard time propagating. This would create the right technological revolution and a new economic system that can integrate and support all nations simultaneously. This kind of collaboration would also help tackle future pandemics like COVID-19 or even mega catastrophic events on Earth or in the far depths of space.

How Would the Outcome of a Mega Space Project Differ from Any Traditional Economic Development Project?

Space Economics may be an answer to some of the conventional economic measures that cannot revive the economy quickly under the current world situation.

Economies of Scale

Small countries cannot compete in economies of scale with industrial giants like China. Additionally, small developing countries cannot cope with advanced technological nations employing extreme automation or using the economies of scope concept smartly. Resourceful and aggressive governments can always limit the economies of scale advantage of weak or developing countries considerably.

Foreign Direct Investment (FDI)

Rivalries among regional and major powers sometimes limit businesses from taking advantage of developing nations' FDI incentives. Fear of regional conflicts, political instabilities, corruption, unfair trade practices, trade wars, tariffs, patriotism, and the rising trend of nationalism are limiting future FDI ventures.

Stimulus Packages

Sometimes, applying the Keynesian Economics Multiplier effect through stimulus packages doesn't produce the expected results when government deficits are high, and the masses have limited buying power. For example, in Pakistan, some economic advisors suggested building five million houses to boost the economy. This may not work with high government deficits, where the majority of the populace does not have real buying power, or where the contractors or business tycoons get the majority of the profits that end up in savings accounts, foreign bank accounts, or stagnant real estate investments at home or abroad.

How to Make It Possible in a Realistic Timeframe

1. **Utilizing Human Resources**
   High unemployment and an abundance of readily available human resources present an opportunity to recruit and rapidly train unskilled labor under various nations' armed forces capabilities and through the oversight of entities like the US/UK "Office of Science and Technology Cooperation" or the "Council of Science and Technology."

2. **Initiating a Mega Collaborative Project**
   This project can become a reality by starting a mega collaborative project in an experimental/entrepreneur-friendly country where high-tier investors like Richard Branson (Virgin Galactic), Elon Musk (SpaceX), and Jeff Bezos (Blue Origin) are given incentives to transform space dreams into reality.

3. **Bold Steps by Any Nation**
   It can even be any country other than the US/UK willing to take the bold step of developing the capability and effectively utilizing their human resources to transform into a knowledge-based economy. Usually, first movers, risk-takers, and creative minds turn a country's tipping scale from developing to developed, creating a ripple effect that transforms surrounding regions from doubt to possibility.

4. **Entrepreneurial and Military Collaboration**
   Entrepreneurs like Richard Branson, Elon Musk, or Jeff Bezos, in collaboration with the combined operational capabilities and discipline of world armed forces, can build a space program facility within months.

5. **Developing Smart Cities**

   Developments like housing complexes, shopping markets, a university, and a recruitment center built around the space program project facility can revive the economy through a multiplier effect. Creating a small city from scratch is less hassle than carving out new developments from old infrastructures. The US and many large countries have ample land and human resources; why not use them boldly and wisely? It would be a new smart city. Consumer trade would automatically jump-start along logistical routes, and a transportation network to and from the smart city would promptly deliver goods and services from day one. The principles of Keynesian economics would automatically come into effect, proving far more practical in reviving the economy than bringing back old manufacturing units or begging investors and corporations to return to their native countries to create employment. Workforce professionals, from laborers, barbers, tailors, cooks, construction workers, scientists, pilots, engineers, architects, teachers, and professors, would start getting immediate employment. The base needed to build a knowledge-based economy would emerge as a byproduct of this project.

6. **Blending Micro-Economics and Social Constructs**

   Offering opportunities to the unemployed and willing populace with high return and national recognition for their contribution would effectively blend micro-economics with the social construct of diverse ethnic backgrounds through collaboration in this mega national project. Developments like suppliers and vendors setting up around project areas and a diverse workforce working for a world project reminiscent of sending Americans to the moon would rewire generational memory, cultural identity, and national pride for a collective win for the state and any dissatisfied populace.

7. **Government and Tech Giant Partnerships**

   Government partnerships with American tech giants can develop the space program's technical capabilities much faster. At this time, offering rivals like China and Russia to join the project would create a synergy effect, speed up the process tremendously, increase the chances of project success, and seal the U.S. image as proactive, collaborative leaders. This space project can bring countries like China, Russia, etc., into a never-before-seen collaboration on purely mutual win-win economic and technical benefits.

8. **Public Communication and Transparency**

   Rapidly completed project milestones communicated to the public and the world would motivate the populace and propagate transparency. Initiatives like time-bound tax incentives and returns on investments to corporations and high-end investors worldwide can attract mega investments to move the project to the next phase quickly.

9. **Leadership and Vision**

   Fortune favors the brave and the first movers. Through a mix of diplomacy, collaboration, and unconventional wits, leadership with guts, wisdom, and resources can transform this impossibility into economic bliss and achieve the next level of technological transformation in the post-COVID-19 era.

10. **Global Unity and Understanding**

    A mega collaborative space project would give a sense of mission and unified direction to the world populace, resulting in understanding each other, tolerance, respecting differences, and accepting diversity and competition in its true essence. As a result, extremism and terrorism would decrease, and the culture of suspicion and conspiracy theories would fade away with progress. Construction of worldwide recruitment and training facilities, and research and development initiatives on a massive scale, may benefit more than war profiteering, drugs, oil, and the porn industry revenues combined.

Conclusion: The Promise of Space Economics

It is time to embrace collaborative economics instead of confrontational economics. Space Economics (S.E.) can provide the ideal platform for global and regional players to unite towards a common goal: creating jobs and driving the next technological revolution. Through collaboration in space, nations can achieve economic prosperity while maintaining their national identities.

Though Space Economics may seem complex and is still in its early stages, it presents a unique opportunity for policymakers to explore something greater than anything before. A significant space project will also kickstart the next wave of manufacturing and the much-needed future industrial revolution, showcasing American ingenuity and leadership, and ultimately stabilizing both the American and global economies.

Today, as humanity faced one of its worst pandemics, regional rivalries—like India vs. Pakistan, Saudi Arabia vs. Iran, and Israel vs. certain Muslim nations, Azerbaijan vs. Armenia—are on the brink of escalation. Tensions over technological dominance between the U.S. and China are brewing into a cold economic war. Businesses are teetering on the edge of chaos, inflation is soaring, people are desperate for jobs, and economies are teetering on the brink of depression.

If anyone has a better idea than Space Economics, now is the time to step forward and share it with the world. Economics is at the heart of our challenges, and it will be at the heart of our solutions. We must act now to start a new beginning that is both achievable and within our reach.

Space Economics Project - To Be Continued...

I discussed a Space Economics project proposal and the following pointers with some academics and influential individuals on how to kickstart the Space Economics wheel within a realistic timeline.

However, I chose not to blend strategic and operational scenarios here. Space Economics isn't just about building spaceships or establishing colonies on the Moon or Mars. There are numerous lucrative, strategic, and impactful benefits on Earth as a result of technological advancement cascade effects on existing industries, and Keynesian Economics and multiplier effects when all the pieces are put together.

Why Hasn't This Been Thought of Before? Traditional mindsets, conventional business models, and shortsighted medieval political and diplomatic views of dominance may not be able to imagine or comprehend the power of this project. Ironically, it also gives more prominence and legitimacy to the U.S. and rival powers. What strategic location can benefit all the major players like the U.S., China, Russia, India, Pakistan, and many others? How can this project become a stepping stone to the next industrial revolution, fostering true peace, creating tremendous employment, and even solving issues like refugees and illegal immigration without blame or loss of face? Which key individuals in the world can make this project a reality within a short, realistic timeline? The world won't see the power of true collaboration and the impact of this project until they start thinking of making the impossible possible.

Who Can Make This Vision a Reality? Can visionaries like Richard Branson, Elon Musk, Jeff Bezos, or others achieve this seemingly impossible task? Could it be someone like Kamala Harris, Trump, Putin, Xi, Erdogan, Crown Prince Mohammed bin Salman Al Saud, or a combined effort from all of them? What would be the most strategic location to bring all these rivals together for a collaboration never seen before? What would be the masterstroke to make this happen? This would be the ultimate political, diplomatic, and entrepreneurial challenge, requiring transparency and an extremely unconventional approach. Will this crown be claimed by a prudent political master or by a bold and unconventional entrepreneur? So, who do you think will dare to take this challenge and become the ultimate legend of all legends?

Hypothetical Scenarios

The First Scenario

Many intellectuals and people around the world perceive China's rising economic strength, the CPEC, and the Chinese One Belt One Road initiatives as irritating to the U.S. and some Western countries. To many, China doesn't want war; they seem interested in economics only until provoked, leaving them with no other option. In another scenario, in one of the most volatile regions, two nuclear powers, India and Pakistan, are always a spark away from an intractable conflict. Pakistani intellectuals think that their old friend America is now anti-Pakistan because of the Pakistan-China friendship and the influence of Israeli and Indian lobbyists (I perceived this feeling among the Pakistani government and people when Imran Khan was Prime Minister). The perception further assumes that U.S. planners intend to instigate a fight between India and China to neutralize China. However, for India to confront China, India must neutralize Pakistan first. When I was trying to publish the first edition of my book, the Ukraine conflict had just started; I wish I could have published this version of the book before that conflict so President Putin could have read it before the Ukraine invasion.

On the other hand, Indians perceive Pakistan as their eternal enemy and an instigator of unrest in Kashmir. Moreover, both countries have large populations, with unemployment issues and economic concerns as ongoing headaches for their leaders. Does space economics offer a solution to a problem like this?

What if an American entrepreneur like Elon Musk or Jeff Bezos, or a British visionary like Richard Branson, could do the impossible by building one of the Space Project's sites at the heart of CPEC and China's One Belt One Road initiative, bringing all the rivals to one platform for a mega collaborative project?

Some people might ask, why not India, Africa, Latin America, or America? The prominent bone of contention is not in India, Africa, Latin America, Europe, or America, but in Baluchistan, the CPEC

(China Pakistan Economic Corridor), and the One Belt One Road Chinese initiative. One must understand that regional and smaller countries usually bear the cost of economic rivalry among superpowers, and the repercussions often extend far beyond the zone of conflict.

What if the perception of rivalry and the resources spent on countering and maligning each other were instead spent on collaborating on a mega space project at a location perceived as an economic threat by a rival? The resources and energy spent on collaboration would take both rivals far ahead, instead of using the same resources to counter each other. What if the rivals become part of that project? American policymakers stress peace and collaboration for a peaceful region between Armenia and Azerbaijan. Why can't the same policymakers look into collaborating with their own rivals too? How about Russians, Americans, and Chinese collaborating on a mega space project?

Would a blunt, fearless businessman, entrepreneur, and leader like Trump make it happen? Would an outspoken, bold Prime Minister like Imran Khan (before his ouster) or the current PM Shahbaz Sharif have the vision to foresee the impact? Would a nationalist icon like Prime Minister Modi have the courage and heart to bring the world's rivals onto a single platform for peace, where one doesn't have to worry about subduing Pakistan or competing with China, but instead becomes part of a bigger game never imagined before? Would President Putin have the guts and foresight to see how Russia can become an integral part of this project, transforming the Russian image from traditional Czars to peacemakers and collaborators in building economies? Would the next U.S. President have the strength and wisdom to make this project the world's first collaborative project among all the rivals on the world's most contentious grounds, just at the corner of Iran and Afghanistan, where rivals might even convince the Taliban to contribute Afghanistan's resources and manpower for this in return for negotiating women's rights and building infrastructure and human capital for the next industrial revolution? There will be enough for everyone in this project. This first space project site can transform the perceived economic threat by some rivals into an enormous opportunity.

Once the first site is established, the collaborators can create other sites from Europe to America, Africa to Latin America, and Australia.

A collaborative Space Project Initiative from an American entrepreneur at the heart of CPEC would not only bring American investment to a volatile region but set an unprecedented example of collaboration, opening strategic trade routes and creating a new economic domain for everyone. An actual free trade market economy would be in the making.

The U.S. is the greatest nation, the most desirable place for the majority, and the world power that influences and impacts most countries. In my analysis, the U.S. and Israel are possibly the two countries that can effectively initiate global peace and an era of prosperity through Space Economics. If the U.S. and Israel open their arms to allies and rivals for a mega space project, the rest of the world will embrace the gesture. Unfortunately, many decision-makers focus more on impossibilities, generational biases, and self-fulfilling prophecies driven by various religious interpretations. The future is an unwritten slate. God the Almighty is not unjust; even if something is written or destined, when one works for it above and beyond and doesn't give up, God the Almighty Himself may change that script to what we want to write. That's why some wise people say first deserve then desire. Only bold leaders, visionaries, and entrepreneurs can make a global mega Space Economics project a reality.

Some people may think I am living in a fantasy world and biased by focusing only on Israel and the U.S. as having the potential to bring true peace and progress to the world, especially after the events in Gaza. However, Israel has a lot to offer, whether in agriculture, technology, or the emerging domain of space exploration.

I remember my father telling me that in the same U.S. where Jews are now highly respected and occupy top positions, in the 1950s, they had a hard time getting jobs. Through hard work and persistence, they changed their image and stature.

If they are that smart, why not utilize tools like peace and collaboration with sincerity to make mega space projects successful and embrace their neighbors? Are they interested in peace and sharing? I believe everyone is interested in peace and a good life. This begins with sincere collaboration on projects like the space initiatives mentioned in this book.

To me, with hard work, a positive attitude, and perseverance, the Jewish minority achieved commanding leverage years later. We need that kind of spirit, resilience, and foresight to get this project off the ground soon. The world envies the U.S. and Israel, and many conspiracy theories suggest that the U.S. and Israel are one entity and not serious about peace. Only the U.S and Israel can prove this wrong by making such a mega collaborative project a reality. Why not the U.S. and Israel put the same effort and enthusiasm into a mega space project with allies and rivals? Instead of focusing on petty world resources, think of the vast resources God made for us to explore and capture throughout the universe.

REFERENCES

Bennett, J. G. a. J. C. (2019). The Economics of Space: An Industry Ready to Launch.

Broad, W. J. (2008). Inside the Black Budget. The New York Times.

FERDINAND, P. (2016). Westward ho—the China dream and 'one belt, one road': Chinese foreign policy under Xi Jinping.

International Affairs, 92(4), 941-957. doi:10.1111/1468-2346.12660

(2019, May 28, 2019). Understanding the space economy [Harvard Business Review - HBR IdeaCast / Episode 684].

Rickards, J. (2011). *Currency Wars.*

Ryan, T. (2020). Space Economics: The Final Frontier.

MANUFACTURING PARADOX, SHORTCUTS, AND COUCH POTATO MENTALITY

I nstead of finding ways to become cost-competitive within our environment, we often take the easy way out by moving to countries like Mexico, Indonesia, Malaysia, and China. We made China bigger than it is, and now we are trying to quarantine the panda bear back into the cage we prefer. The world doesn't always work as we plan and think; otherwise, we would have won in Afghanistan and Vietnam, and things would have gone our way in places like Iraq, Syria, and Libya. When Deming introduced the TQM (Total Quality Management) concept, our corporate leaders didn't take him as seriously as the Japanese did. Ultimately, the Japanese used an American's ideas to turn their auto manufacturing around, eventually competing with and surpassing American automakers.

Instead of perfecting our manufacturing through technology and concepts like advanced Total Quality Management (TQM) to gain a price and quality competitive advantage over rivals like China, our traditional CEOs outsourced manufacturing units and even service jobs like call centers. Instead of thinking about how to use machine learning, AI, robotics, economies of scale, and economies of scope to our advantage, many CEOs took the easy way out so that they had more time for golf. By the way, who pays these CEOs excessive compensation packages for closing our manufacturing units and outsourcing our jobs? Does anyone ever look deeply at what is going on? I guess, the top and the rich have only three minutes or three lines of stamina.

Some say we are becoming a services-oriented society; I think that's also not entirely true because I see many banking, insurance, and other service and call centers in India, the Philippines, and other countries. For some quick bucks, our lobbyists and corporate heads convinced our policymakers to move our manufacturing facilities to other countries. Instead of making our manufacturing more price-competitive and quality-oriented by focusing on new methodologies and research and development, we abandoned manufacturing completely. To save labor costs, we even moved our customer service and call centers to other countries.

Unintentionally, our policymakers are transforming our talented, innovative, and potential-filled populace into a manufacture-less and service-less society. Most of our compatriots are becoming consumers who just pay, live paycheck to paycheck, buy cheaper products, find shortcuts, buy insurance, and subconsciously transform into a fearful and litigious culture.

Instead of becoming creative, forgiving, and understanding, we are turning into an impatient, shortsighted, selfish, emotional society. Some are becoming angry and jealous of others' success. Some of us see immigrants from India, Korea, Yemen, and Mexico getting ahead and think they are taking our businesses and jobs. These legal immigrants are working hard and united – if they can make it, why can't other Americans? Instead of blaming others and crying over their successes, why don't we start using common sense?

Get Off the Couch and Switch On Life: We made Japan, Germany, and South Korea stronger, and now we are making China stronger. What is China? If the American public stops buying Chinese products and Walmart and Amazon stop buying Chinese products, the Chinese will have a hard time running their factories. Chinese are not getting ahead – we are standing still or deteriorating. Once this U.S. giant, the fearless eagle, rises, China and the world will know what the American spirit and capabilities are. We are sleeping.

Why are Walmart and Amazon not manufacturing here in America now? Why not put their profits into finding ways to give our products and services a competitive advantage over our rivals? Why do Walmart and Amazon not consider U.S. competitiveness and national interests over their corporate profits? Why do these corporations and lobbyists not think of America first? These corporations and lobbyists will reap what they sow. Do they want to give Americans and their future generations an America without manufacturing and even without a service sector, with the majority living on paychecks and their children becoming subservient to Chinese and other rivals?

Revive the American Spirit: Freedom doesn't come free, and we cannot ignore the cost of maintaining it. We are underestimating our potential by giving up our manufacturing, outsourcing our jobs, and believing we cannot compete with cheap Chinese products. Don't settle for less; instead of thinking about becoming a vulture, be that American eagle we are proud to be. There is no easy way out; there are no shortcuts. We must return to the master's mode, not the mediocre mode. Embrace the competition and show the world we can do better. Think about possibilities instead of impossibilities. Don't go after cheap – be American, buy American.

Don't Underestimate Your Potential: Where is your patriotism, integrity, humility, creativity, and common sense, my compatriots? Since we started worrying about China, we gave in to the logic that we cannot compete with Chinese manufacturing on price and quantities. I would call those economists not even average who would say I may not know labor costs, raw material costs, behind-the-scenes issues, and how economies of scale work. I know how it works, and I also know that we Americans are capable of using AI, machine learning, advanced TQM, and futuristic quantum automation to our favor to get that competitive advantage we need. Since when did we start giving up, and who are those consultants and CEOs who go for shortcuts and think U.S. corporate profitability is different from American national interests?

Our corporate gurus got rid of manufacturing and now services. What's next? What are our intelligent and experienced decision-makers up to? Believe it or not, people worldwide still like American-made products and are willing to pay more for quality American products, which last much longer than cheap short-term Chinese products. So, who was that shortsighted consultant who suggested abandoning manufacturing because we couldn't compete on price? We are Americans, and the American spirit and creativity can prove its mettle again by making high-price products cheaper through technology, advanced TQM, and extending product life cycles.

Move Forward from Past Grievances: Some of our compatriots cannot move past grievances. I know it is hard, but as a nation, we need to move forward. Even when we protest, we sometimes break our own compatriots' shops and businesses. Instead of target protesting the culprits and letting our justice system work, we try to take justice into our hands and also become little culprits, losing our credibility, cause, and a winning case to media mockery. We are becoming soft, and then we complain about how our allies are not united. How can our allies be united when we at home are not united? For God's sake, put your differences aside, and don't let other nations take advantage of you. Don't make a mockery of yourself. Unity, faith, and discipline make nations great, not the other way around.

Lift Each Other Up: Instead of becoming creative, supportive, and finding ways, we criticize and fight with each other. First, deserve, then desire.

Where is the leader who will genuinely unite us? America is second to none, and who will wear the next crown?

President Trump, can you this time prove everyone wrong by uniting the nation and implementing common-sense ideas from this book?

Are you and your base up for the challenge?

DO WE REALLY
UNDERSTAND KARMA?

We often talk about Karma, and most of us have heard sayings like, "what goes around comes around," and "fool me once, shame on you; fool me twice, shame on me."

I once met a friend whose business partner had cheated him. My friend told me he left justice in the hands of God, believing in the saying, "if you leave your worries and planning to God, then God takes care of your worries because He is the best of planners." But my friend's wife didn't buy into this idea of Karma or divine planning. She insisted, "if Karma were that effective, we wouldn't need lawyers and courts." She had an interesting point.

On the other hand, my friend had a different perspective. He said, "people and world powers underestimate Karma and God's justice. People don't usually realize how Karma works and how it comes back to them. For instance, my business partner who deceived me—his wife left him, he developed a heart problem, then cancer, and his other business ventures failed. Sure, I lost some money, but I have healthy kids, a loving wife who doesn't believe in Karma :), and a regret-free, peaceful life."

The workings of Karma aren't always obvious, and many don't understand it. Karma isn't as straightforward as a math equation. Those who commit wrongs often find Karma striking in unexpected ways, robbing them of contentment and peace. We don't need to be the world's policemen; we need to fix our own house first. Let other countries, with their unique norms and cultures, develop through their own learning curves. Let's focus on our success and improving our homeland; when others see our progress and unmatched achievements, they'll want to join us on the train of progress.

Instead of constantly worrying about others, let's worry about ourselves. My friend believes Karma doesn't work linearly to settle scores but rather operates in a more quantum manner, settling things in ways most people don't understand. I often reflect on what my friend told me and observe the world around me. Sometimes, Karma's timelines extend beyond a few years, affecting generations. Only those who can connect the dots truly comprehend Karma's consequences.

In the end, I leave it to you, the reader, to decide how God and Karma work.

A GLIMPSE INTO MY NEXT BOOK: TACKLING AMERICA'S DRUG PROBLEM, SUE CULTURE, AND A REVOLUTIONARY MORTGAGE THEORY

Revolutionizing Home Ownership: An Interest-Free Mortgage Theory

In my next book, if God the Almighty permits, I will introduce the idea of an Interest-Free Mortgage Theory revolution. Imagine an America where foreclosures are a thing of the past, and an average family can own their home in less time without piling up debt. This can be achieved through an interest-free, stock market-driven mortgage model that allows buyers and sellers to trade homes as commodities by equating house values to shares. This innovative approach could also stabilize our stock market by tying shares to tangible assets like land. The potential economic and societal benefits could be enormous, making the mortgage market lucrative for both investors and buyers. While banks reliant on high-interest rates might resist, this model promises to modernize the mortgage process and significantly improve the lives of millions of Americans, creating an economically sustainable and socially responsible mortgage system.

Addressing the Drug Epidemic: A Common-Sense Approach

Despite extensive research and numerous government measures, the drug problem in America isn't going away—in fact, it's getting worse. Are we missing a simple, common-sense approach? Have we lost the old American way of doing things—the simple and right way? Using common sense, I see a pattern: people often start with cigarettes, then move to marijuana, and eventually harder drugs. Their motivation is usually down; they're stressed, overworked, and don't see hope. They need relaxation or energy. Instead of letting our youth get lost in video games, why not engage them in sports in a meaningful way?

If I had the power, I would humbly request our policymakers and leaders to read an excellent book, "8 Hidden Commandments Champions Don't Violate: Now You Have Them to Achieve Your DIVINITY in Sports" by Mohammad Asim. This book should be a mandatory curriculum book in sports. In his book and podcasts, he reveals how the concept of Citius, Altius, Fortius (Faster, Higher, Stronger) can be used to train and motivate our youth, keeping them off drugs before they even start. Let's empower our youth through sports and give them something meaningful to do—the old American way. By doing so, we can address the root causes of drug addiction and create a healthier, more engaged society.

The Sue Culture: Can Common Sense Restore American Values and Business Integrity?

In today's America, our sue culture is unraveling the very fabric of our values—respect and the spirit of helping others. This pervasive culture, where laws meant to safeguard us have spiraled out of control, allows many to get rich quickly by exploiting the system. It's as if the suing culture has armed some lawyers, turning the law into a business, stripping it of its essence as a guardian of safety and justice. Now, everything is driven by ulterior motives and the pursuit of quick wealth.

This not only hurts businesses but also empowers insurance companies to thrive at the expense of the very people the laws were meant to protect. Imagine running a small business, only to be blindsided by a frivolous lawsuit that drains your resources—not to mention the time it takes to do the paperwork to defend yourself. Or think about paying ever-rising insurance premiums because the system is flooded with many baseless claims. This isn't just about legal battles; it's about everyday Americans facing the consequences of a broken system.

However, it's important to acknowledge that when used appropriately, the sue culture is crucial for holding individuals and corporations accountable. Many lawsuits are legitimate and serve to protect the rights of those who have been wronged. Yet, there must be checks and balances. The sue culture shouldn't be a shotgun approach used indiscriminately. We need a balance—protecting individual rights while preventing excessive litigation. It's about fostering a society that values cooperation, common sense, and mutual respect, all while ensuring justice and accountability.

In the end, we find ourselves in a society where the spirit of cooperation and mutual respect is overshadowed by opportunism and legal exploitation. The common sense that once guided us seems lost. How did we end up in this mess, and what can we do to reclaim our values and common sense? Let's start by rethinking the way we approach lawsuits and strive for a system that truly serves justice, respects human dignity, and fosters a cooperative, respectful community.

A World Without Borders: A Bold Vision for the Future

Though the book "World With No Visa" may seem too futuristic, it envisions a world where people travel without visas, with a system that recognizes everyone's identity and place of origin by their looks

119

and speech. Before borders existed, people moved freely, and in a true free-market economy, this should be possible again, resolving the issue of illegal immigration.

Some might argue that this vision is unrealistic, citing current issues like terrorism and security concerns. However, if we address the root causes of problems like the refugee crisis and wars, my Space Economics article could be the first step towards this future. In a world where people can work wherever they find jobs and pay taxes to both local and origin governments, the challenges of illegal immigration and finding the right workers would be resolved. Why not embrace this visionary approach and start solving these issues at their core?

This next book aims to provide practical solutions and visionary ideas that tackle America's most pressing issues. By addressing the drug epidemic, reforming our sue culture, revolutionizing home ownership, and envisioning a world without borders, we can create a better, more just society for all.

Note: I greatly appreciate suggestions, constructive critiques, and feedback on this book. I welcome discussions on topics not covered here but which may be included in future editions.

I HAVE A DREAM TOO

I have some dreams and wishes too.

I have a dream that bold policymakers make Space Economics a reality, rooted in true peace and collaboration. Visionaries and entrepreneurs like Elon Musk can make this happen in record time, beyond what the world could imagine. I dream of visiting colonies on Mars that Elon envisions, because I believe this is possible.

I have a dream that instead of seeing the One Belt One Road initiative as competition or threat, we use it and the CPEC for the most extensive collaboration and employment generation the world has ever seen. And I dream that U.S. policymakers are the ones to make rivals like Russia, China, India, Pakistan, and others work together. Only an American mind can think of these possibilities.

I have a dream of seeing Palestinians and Israelis working side by side, preparing to go as a team in a spaceship to build Elon Musk's Mars colony and beyond.

I have a dream that peace prevails between Azerbaijan and Armenia, and there is a tourist and commercial train service connecting Georgia, Azerbaijan, Armenia, Turkey, Iraq, Saudi Arabia, Syria, Israel, Egypt, and many other countries, fostering tourism, trade, peace, and collaboration. Trains would take skilled labor from the Caucasus to Elon's space platform, transporting people to build colonies on Mars and beyond.

I have a dream that places around the world, especially in Africa and Latin America, become space platforms, learning centers, tourist

121

hubs, and innovation centers where world citizens visit to enjoy peace, greenery, serenity, and exchange ideas.

I have a dream that instead of putting criminals and drug dealers in jail and making them more dangerous, instead of sidelining fanatics and making them more extreme, policymakers devise policies and programs that channel these individuals' energies and creativity into building logistics networks, space colonies, and making the next industrial revolution successful in half the time.

Some policymakers may laugh reading this because they lack the vision to comprehend or the operational knowledge to connect the dots, but visionaries, bold leaders, and unconventional entrepreneurs can make these dreams realities in our lifetime.

ENDING ON A DEDICATION NOTE

I dedicate this book, first and foremost, to all my fellow Americans, especially those who feel frustrated and worried about the current state of affairs. I also dedicate it to all my loved ones and friends, particularly my parents, children, brother and sisters, and their families, and those who prayed for me and for this book's success. Thank you for your continuous support and encouragement in making this happen. To my children – I love you all dearly.

I want to express my gratitude to my mentors and teachers who enabled me to imagine, think, and write about impossibilities. Special thanks to my previous bosses from the US State Department, the Defense Language Institute – US Department of Defense, and my university professors for helping me improve my writing skills. I truly believe that if I hadn't worked at the US State Department, I couldn't write as I do now. A special tribute goes to my father's friend, Ajmal Shah, who, along with my father, encouraged me to write this book and polish my Space Economics article and not give up. Thanks to Sabahat for fixing my cover page for this second edition amidst all the distractions and interruptions. Thanks to my friends Tareen and Honorable George Bailey for listening to my discussions on my book's points and giving me some common sense, which gave me the motivation and clarity to write this book. Additionally, thanks to John Register for proofreading and offering thoughts.

This book aims to address issues dividing our society using common sense and to explore different perspectives on current events in America. It also discusses a project that offers hope and the potential to generate tremendous employment.

I dedicate this book to people worldwide who have always admired America's strong institutions, transparent justice system, and commitment to upholding the law and its constitution. These individuals believe the world can learn from the American experience to improve their own countries. Yet, they are sometimes disheartened to see Americans divided and struggling with internal challenges.

I dedicate this book to our children and future generations, urging them to look beyond the limitations of our current world and envision possibilities our forefathers could only dream of. Our ancestors provided us with a beautiful, resource-rich, free homeland, a launching pad for even greater achievements. Our future should be one of hope, possibilities, and a brighter tomorrow.

I hope this book sparks logic and understanding among Americans, leading to solutions for the issues that divide us. This book is not advocating for American isolationism but emphasizes that we must fix our own house first before we can effectively help others. America has always been a beacon of hope for the world; we must ensure we remain strong to continue this legacy.

Finally, I dedicate this book to policymakers and those in power. I hope they approach the ideas with an open mind, open heart, and a spirit of innovation. I believe in their ability to listen, welcome critique, and take steps to improve our homeland. Unlike others, we Americans focus on possibilities rather than impossibilities, which makes mega collaborative projects like Space Economics a potential reality. This mindset is what sets us apart and makes us truly American.

ABOUT THE AUTHOR

The author has a Ph.D. in Computing and Information Systems, with an extensive and multifaceted career in both corporate and government sectors. Among many roles, his remarkable journey includes positions such as Chief Operating Officer, Director of Operations, General Manager, Deputy Director, Economic Specialist, Professional Associate, Academic Specialist, Assistant Professor, and Math Teacher. With over 20 years of diverse international experience, he has excelled in research, academics, operations, as well as project and program management. His expertise spans machine learning, complexity, data analysis, and economic reporting and analysis, garnered from working with prestigious institutions like the US State Department, the US Department of Defense, and the corporate world. This diverse international experience assures readers of his global perspective.

Among other achievements, he is also the recipient of the Commander's Award for Civilian Service and the Achievement Medal for Civilian Service. Moreover, he led the US Embassy Baku Green Team that won the 2022 Greening Diplomacy Initiative (GDI) Award for Excellence in Team Sustainability Performance.

His multifaceted career also includes stints as a Management Consultant for industrial partners, Finance Manager of a technology incubation center, Lead Project Manager for a consulting firm, and Business Analyst for a tech company. His impressive academic credentials, including an MBA and bachelor's degrees in Business, Economics, Statistics, and Mathematics, attest to his deep knowledge and expertise. He has also completed the POLECON Tradecraft Course from the US Foreign Service Institute, the Instructor Course Certification from the US Defense Language Institute, and received a Hospitality Management Program Certification from Wyndham University, further broadening his skill set. Combined with his economic and regional expertise, these qualifications provide him with unparalleled insight and a unique perspective, giving additional credibility and firepower to this unconventional book's blunt and unique perspective.

In his previous edition, he initially wanted to title the book "Where is the FKN Commonsense?" but was advised by a mentor to avoid slang and focus on the concept of Space Economics. He thus named it "A Commonsense Book with a Trillion Dollar Project," while still hinting at his original title on the cover and writing under the pen name "You and Me" to eliminate bias. Due to overwhelming encouragement from friends and feedback from some readers, he has reverted to his original title in this second edition, proudly displaying his name and credentials. The title, "Where is the FKN Commonsense?" captures his candid, thought-provoking style, offering readers a refreshing, no-nonsense, enlightening, and transformative perspective.

(Author - Mohammad Asif Nawaz)

Printed in the United States
by Baker & Taylor Publisher Services